CONTRARY
INVESTING

CONTRARY INVESTING:

The Insider's Guide to Buying Low & Selling High

RICHARD E. BAND

McGRAW-HILL BOOK COMPANY
New York St. Louis San Francisco
Toronto Hamburg Mexico

To Enid, who kept me on track.

2 3 4 5 6 7 8 9 D O C D O C 8 7 6 5

ISBN 0-07-003604-7

LIBRARY OF CONGRESS CATALOGING IN PUBLICATION DATA

Band, Richard E.
   Contrary investing.
   Bibliography: p.
   Includes index.
   1. Investments—Handbooks, manuals, etc.
2. Speculation—Handbooks, manuals, etc.   I. Title.
HG4527.B233   1985   332.6'78   85-99
ISBN 0-07-003604-7

BOOK DESIGN BY PATRICE FODERO

Contents

Graphs

Acknowledgments

A book is the product of many hands, and I cheerfully acknowledge my debt to those who had a hand in this one. First of all, I wish to thank my boss at KCI Communications, Brian W. Smith, who encouraged me to undertake this project, and Clare Matthews, his dedicated assistant, who pressed me to complete it. Renee Deprey, Diane Sterman, John Chaiyakul, and Jamie Familio in the KCI art department were of incalculable help in preparing the charts and graphs.

To the many outstanding contrary thinkers in the investment community from whom I have learned—Donald J. Hoppe, Douglas R. Casey, Ian McAvity, David Dreman, James Fraser, and Earl Hadady, among others—I offer the gratitude of a dwarf mounted upon the shoulders of giants. I must also express my appreciation for the work of the late Humphrey Neill, who coined the term "contrary opinion" and first elucidated the subject in print. Yale Hirsch, publisher of *The Stock Trader's Almanac*, provided me with several of the quotations that appear at the beginning of the chapters.

In a sense, this book has been brewing in my head since childhood. My father, Hans E. Band, and Myron H. Ferrin, an early spiritual counselor, deserve thanks for teaching me to distrust the fads and follies of the crowd. Mr. Ferrin's rule that "the majority is seldom right" has stood me in good stead.

I am grateful to Neil McCaffrey, president of the Conservative Book Club, for the many insights he has shared with me about good writing. I am also indebted to my friend Mark Skousen, who coaxed me out of the womb of a big Boston bank and persuaded me to take "the road less traveled by." That has made all the difference.

Finally, to all those who offered me encouragement while I was slogging through the manuscript, my thanks: to all the staff of KCI, especially my colleagues Adrian Day and Frederic Cochard, to the Reverend Mark and Gwenyth Oien, and to my nagging, cajoling, supporting, and understanding wife, Enid, who more than anyone else made the completion of the task possible.

CONTRARY
INVESTING

1
The Billionaire's Secret

Buy when everyone else is selling, and hold until everyone
else is buying. This is more than just a catchy slogan. It is
the very essence of successful investment.
—J. Paul Getty
How to Be Rich

Oil tycoon J. Paul Getty was probably the wealthiest man who ever
lived. When he died in 1976 at the age of 83, Getty presided over a
business empire that embraced nearly 200 companies, with the Getty
Oil Co. as the crown jewel. He owned an elegant Tudor mansion in
southern England and had amassed one of the world's great art collec-
tions. His personal fortune was worth an estimated $3 billion.

Was Getty just lucky, or did he know something the rest of us don't?
In his autobiography, he conceded that a little bit of bloomin' luck
certainly helped. But, like all great entrepreneurs, Getty also understood
the power of contrary thinking. Early on, he discovered what I call "the
billionaire's secret": If you want to make money—the big money—do
what nobody else is doing. Find the niches that nobody else is filling.
Look for overlooked opportunities. In baseball parlance, "Hit 'em where
they ain't." J. Paul Getty knew that you can often snare the best profits
by putting capital into ventures that most investors either haven't heard
about or are too afraid to touch.

Successful business people grasp this principle almost by instinct.
People dismissed Henry Ford as an illiterate handyman when his first
two-cylinder roadster putt-putted out of the shop in 1896. But the joke
was actually on the scoffers—the blacksmiths and harnessmakers who
were trapped in conventional thinking, unable to foresee the vast po-

tential market for the automobile. Thirty years later, Ford was a multimillionaire and nobody laughed.

To take a more recent case, most observers of the computer industry in the mid-1970s confidently predicted that it would take a long time—maybe ten or fifteen years—before a mass market would open up for personal computers. The existing machines were too costly for retail merchandising and too complex for Mr. and Mrs. America to operate.

One fledgling outfit, Apple Computer, challenged the consensus. Founded by a 21-year-old engineering whiz kid, Steven Jobs, literally in his garage, Apple turned out a series of low-cost, "user-friendly" microcomputers that almost anyone with a grade school education could learn to operate. In less than a decade, the company has grown from nothing to $1 billion in annual sales. Meanwhile, it has spawned a host of competitors—most notably IBM—who suddenly discovered that there was indeed a mass market for personal computers.

Think for Yourself

Contrary thinking is the art of thinking for yourself against the pressures of the crowd. The contrary investor, like J. Paul Getty, buys assets that others are rushing to sell, and sells assets that others are clamoring to buy. He isn't trying to be ornery or eccentric; he merely recognizes that if *nobody* wants something, it is likely to be cheap. If *everybody* wants it, it is likely to be dear. Contrary thinking is probably the simplest, sanest, and most reliable technique that has ever been devised to buy low and sell high—for maximum profit. In fact, I would argue that every successful investor is a contrarian at heart, whether he recognizes it or not.

You can apply a contrary strategy to any investment market, from stocks and bonds to precious metals, commodities, foreign currencies, real estate, collectibles—you name it. As it turns out, however, most of the existing books on contrary investing (only a handful have been written over the past thirty years) focus narrowly on one market, usually the stock market. I take a different tack. In today's volatile economy, I think it is essential to keep your mind open to all markets, even if as a practical matter you can't (and shouldn't try to) participate in all of them. This book will show you how to profit by "going against the crowd" in any market you choose.

Contrary thinking works in any market because human nature is the same everywhere. Most people are followers, not leaders. In the marketplace, they wait to buy until they see other people buying, and they wait to sell until they see other people selling. As a result, most people buy after prices have already risen, and sell after prices have already fallen. (Some investment analysts—so-called technical analysts—have raised this type of behavior to an art form; they prefer, though, to call it trend following rather than what it really is: crowd following.)

By chasing the crowd, the typical investor loses profits at both ends: he buys too high and sells too low. On the other hand, if you learn to recognize the extremes of crowd psychology, you can go *against* the crowd when signs of a manic top or a panic bottom appear. Of course, I don't promise that you will always hit the exact top or bottom; statistically, such a feat is next to impossible. But with a contrary strategy, you can buy closer to the bottom (or sell closer to the top). In short, you can capture a larger share of the profits to be made from any significant market move.

Some of the techniques I describe in this book will appeal primarily to sophisticated investors—the type who enjoy burrowing through the *Wall Street Journal* with calculator in hand. However, I want to stress at the outset that you don't need an advanced degree in economics or finance to practice the art of contrary thinking. As a matter of fact, you can become a successful contrarian simply by reading between the lines of your daily newspaper.

What you do need is the ability to control your emotions and think calmly when everyone else in the marketplace is verging on hysteria. More than brains, contrary investing takes self-discipline and an ounce of courage. But these aren't superhuman virtues; anybody with an independent streak can learn to be a contrary thinker. In fact, if you have ever been labeled a maverick or a boat rocker, or simply a lone wolf, you may already be a practicing contrarian without even knowing it!

People Make Markets

The theory of contrary opinion, as it is formally called, is based squarely on the fact that *people make markets*. Even in this age of electronic wizardry, people—not computers—still make the final decision to buy or sell anything, from stocks and bonds to automobiles, teddy bears, and brussels sprouts. A market, after all, is merely a collection of *people* buying and selling.

However, there are two sides to every person. You and I are rational human beings. We think, we plan, we calculate. Reason is what enabled the human race to put a man on the moon, splice genes in the laboratory, and build Pac-Man video games. But we are also emotional creatures who go through moods of hope and despair, confidence and fear, joy and anger, satisfaction and yearning, pride and greed, and a hundred other feelings that only a professional psychologist could begin to catalog.

When a group of people get together to trade stocks, gold or any other investment asset, we create a market that, like us, has a two-sided character, both rational and emotional. The market is rational in the sense that it "sees" (takes notice of) every scrap of information known to investors great or small. The gold market, for example, knows the rate of inflation in every country, the level of interest rates here and abroad, the supply of newly mined metal coming to market, the dimensions of Third World debt crisis (to the extent that anybody really knows), and many other factors that help determine the price of gold. The market is even aware of all the predictions that all the pundits have made about gold. If a fresh piece of information hits the market— say, that Zimbabwe just dropped an atomic bomb on South Africa's largest gold mine—investors will bid the price of gold up or down (most likely *up* in this case) to reflect the new reality.

The truly liquid investment markets (stocks, bonds, precious metals, and commodities) absorb new information amazingly fast. Within minutes after a company releases a bad earnings report, for instance, the price of its stock can plunge 20 or 30 percent. As academics are fond of saying, the stock market, like the gold market or the commodity markets, is an "efficient" (rational) price-setting mechanism. It adjusts prices almost instantaneously to take account of new developments.

However, while the market knows everything that *has* happened, it doesn't know everything that is *going to happen*. The future is uncertain, risky. No individual this side of eternity knows exactly what the economic future will bring, and neither does any group of individuals (the market). In fact, prices change precisely because things happen that the market didn't expect! Surprises make the market go up and down.

The price you pay for an ounce of gold reflects the market's expectations about the future value of gold, based on historical information. But emotion always colors the market's expectations because economic value is in the eye of the beholder. Nobody has a scientific formula that proves conclusively what price gold (or anything else) ought to sell for. Some people think the stuff is worthless; others wouldn't part with their hoard for $2000 an ounce.

To a large extent, the current price of any asset depends on how strongly investors *feel* that current supply-and-demand trends will continue. I may believe, on the basis of my reading of the monetary statistics, that the Federal Reserve is returning to an inflationary policy that will drive up the price of gold. Another analyst reading the same statistics might come to the opposite conclusion.

The statistics don't lie. But my fellow analyst and I draw different inferences from the numbers because he or she puts greater faith than I do in the integrity of the Federal Reserve Board and the willingness of the American political system to accept a clean break with inflation. Both of us are making personal, subjective, *emotional* judgments. And our judgments, along with those of thousands of other market participants, shape the price of gold.

The Myopic Market

In the short term, the market's expectations usually come true. The stock market, for example, is considered a "leading" economic indicator because stock prices generally begin to rise several months before the economy pulls out of a recession and start to fall several months before the economy peaks.

Think back to the summer of 1982, when the Dow Jones industrial average tumbled to a two-year low of 777. What did the stock market see on the horizon? Despite the rosy forecasts of many professional economists, slumping stock prices were saying that investors expected the economy to weaken further for at least the next few months. And the market was correct: the recession deepened for four months after the stock market hit bottom.

However, for any investor who had the foresight to look beyond the next few months, the Dow at 777 was ridiculously undervalued. The market was right about the short-term outlook for the economy, but *totally wrong* about the longer-term outlook. What the market couldn't see in the summer of 1982 was that the nation's central bank was embarking on an "easy money" policy that would eventually spark a powerful economic upswing. Needless to say, the market quickly changed its mind as the shape of the recovery became apparent to most investors. By June 1983, only ten months after the lows, the Dow had soared 61 percent—one of the steepest advances on record.

Every investment market, no matter how rational, suffers from an incurable case of shortsightedness. The long-term bond market is a classic example. For thirty-five years (1946 to 1981), bond buyers doggedly loaned out their money at interest rates that turned out to be too low to compensate for inflation over the life of the bonds. Had bondholders been able to foresee the rapid inflation that began in the mid-1960s, they would never have allowed the Treasury to borrow their money in 1946 at 2 percent interest.

Why were the bondholders repeatedly fooled? They made the mistake of assuming that inflation and interest rates would remain indefinitely at (or near) the level that prevailed when the bonds were issued. Bond buyers projected existing trends far into the future.

For a while, perhaps even for four or five years, the supposition looked good. Interest rates stayed above the inflation rate, and bondholders earned a real return. But in the long run, the bond buyers' projections proved disastrously wrong. Investors weren't stupid. They simply fell prey to the all-too-human tendency to believe that good times (in this case, low interest rates) will go on forever. Complacency— an emotional weakness—clouded their judgment.

The market has a good record for anticipating short-term economic developments, but not for predicting the long term. The longer the time horizon, the less likely that the market can foresee what will happen with any degree of accuracy. Too many variables can intervene to throw the market's assessment off.

Yet, ironically, even though the long run is inherently unpredictable, the market's *long-term* expectations determine the largest part of the price you pay for any investment asset. When you buy a share of IBM for $125, for instance, you are purchasing a claim on the company's assets, earnings, and dividends for as long as IBM is in business. Only a small part of your purchase price reflects the company's near-term prospects; most of the $125 is for a piece of the company's growth into the distant future.

But if nobody has the foggiest idea what IBM will be worth in the distant future, how can the market put a rational price on a share of IBM stock? The obvious answer is that it can't. Part of the price you pay for a share of IBM is rational and part is psychological (or emotional). The short-term component of the market price is rational because the market knows pretty much what IBM's earnings will look like for the next quarter or two, perhaps even for the next year or two. But the long-term component, which carries by far the greater weight, depends almost entirely on investor psychology.

If investors feel supremely confident about IBM's long-range future, they may bid the price of the stock up to forty times the current year's earnings, as they did in early 1973. On the other hand, if investors feel discouraged about the company's long-term prospects, they may trade the stock at only eight times current earnings, as in late 1981. Was IBM a worse company in 1981 than in 1973? Not at all. IBM's earnings, dividends, and book value had soared in those eight-odd years. (In fact, IBM's profits grew *faster* during that period than in the late 1960s and early 1970s.) But investor psychology had shifted dramatically. Investors had soured on IBM.

The Mood of the Market

Understanding the psychological climate of the marketplace is the key to contrary investing. Just as individuals go through a spectrum of moods, so does the market. (Remember, the market is composed of people!) The contrary investor is really an amateur psychologist who tries to *identify the mood of the market*—and profit from it.

When prices are rising, the market's mood turns increasingly optimistic. Investors who bought earlier feel good about their paper profits. New investors who are impressed with the track record decide to buy, believing that the trend will continue. The opposite happens when prices are falling: the market's mood grows increasingly pessimistic. Investors who are sitting on losses feel gloomy, even desperate. New investors are afraid to touch an investment that has been faltering (even though, at important market turning points, past performance tends to be exactly the reverse of future performance).

Economists and philosophers may argue endlessly over whether the mood of the market changes prices, or whether price changes alter the mood of the market. For the investor, it doesn't really matter. The important thing is that the mood of the market rises (and falls) more or less in step with prices. As prices change, the mood of the market changes.

7

Most markets—like the economy as a whole—climb in a jagged pattern for several years at a time (primary bull markets), then fall irregularly for another couple of years (primary bear markets). A primary bull market is characterized by rising prices and growing optimism—not every day or every week, of course, but over a period of many weeks and months. Likewise, falling prices and growing pessimism characterize a primary bear market.

A bull market begins to rise in a climate of *fear*. Later, as the market scores additional gains, fear recedes and an attitude of *caution* takes over in most investors' minds. After prices have climbed substantially, investors start to forget the bad old days of the bear market. *Confidence* reigns. Finally, as prices reach a cyclical peak, *euphoria* sweeps the market. At the top, all but a handful of investors are convinced that the market will keep going up indefinitely.

On the way down, the same emotions predominate, but in reverse order: first euphoria, then confidence, then caution, then fear. At the bottom of the bear market, nearly everyone believes that prices will drop even further.

Contrary investors follow the maxim: "Buy into extreme weakness and sell into extreme strength." They buy when the market is enveloped in fear—and prices are low. They sell when the market is gushing with euphoria—and prices are high. In between, they sit still and let the market do its work.

Within a primary bull or bear trend, there are many secondary reactions *against* the trend lasting for a few days, weeks or even months. In the stock market, for example, prices may fall sharply—even during a strong primary uptrend—for three to five weeks at a time. A rally will then usually ensue, followed by another short-term "correction." If a series of short-term corrections carry prices to successively lower lows, market analysts will often describe the entire period of declining prices as an intermediate-term correction in a bull market.

Corrections are necessary to restore the market's psychological balance when the primary trend pushes prices too far, too fast. In a rapidly climbing bull market, investor sentiment can shift from fear to euphoria in two or three months. By the same token, in a plunging bear market, investor psychology may lurch from euphoria to fear in just a few months. At these short-term or intermediate-term extremes, the market typically undergoes a reaction in the opposite direction, which clears away the excessive optimism or pessimism and sets the stage for the primary trend to continue.

Investors with a long-term point of view can use contrary opinion to spot turning points in the primary trend. However, as I will show in subsequent chapters, contrary thinking is also a helpful tool for identifying intermediate-term and even short-term market peaks and bottoms. Whether you consider yourself a long-term investor or a short-term trader, contrary opinion can sharpen your timing and enhance your profits.

The Madding Crowd

If you consistently buy into fear and sell into euphoria (or greed), you will make money. It sounds easy. But in practice, people seldom do it. When everyone else is afraid that prices are going to crash, we tend to be afraid too. When everyone else is thrilled with the market, the excitement tends to rub off on us too. Most of us don't like to stand alone, clinging to an opinion that nearly everyone else seems to disagree with.

How many dissenters spoke up at the crucifixion of Christ? How many Michigan football fans dare to boo Notre Dame—from a seat in the enemy's grandstands? Our most cherished convictions often melt in the heat of a crowd. Yet it is precisely when the pull of the crowd is strongest that the market makes its most dramatic reversals.

If you have ever attended a sporting event, a political rally, or some other mob scene, you have seen the herd mentality in action. *Unanimity* and *hysteria* are the telltale marks of a crowd. Given the first condition, the second is seldom far behind.

A fire breaks out in a crowded theater. One thought instantly races through everyone's mind: "I must get out at all costs." A moment later, unanimity breeds panic as everyone realizes that everyone else is thinking the same thing. People say to themselves: "If I let the others go first, I may not get out alive." Although this fear may be completely irrational, everybody rushes for the exits simultaneously. Some are crushed to death in the stampede and, ironically, the hall empties more slowly than it might have, because of the congestion at the doors.

People do things in a crowd that they wouldn't think of doing if they were acting as isolated individuals. When I was growing up, my father used to regale me with stories about his classmates at Harvard who, as part of their initiation into the Hasty Pudding Club (a prestigious senior society), rolled pancakes through the streets of bustling Harvard Square at five o'clock in the afternoon. Callow youth that I was, I couldn't believe that "big kids" behaved that way. But they did, and as far as I know, still do.

Nobody over 30 years of age can forget the Beatlemania of the 1960s, when teenage girls screamed, fainted, and broke into convulsions during the rock-and-roll quartet's concerts. A whole generation of men—some of whom didn't especially care for Beatles music—adopted the mop-headed hairstyle made popular by John, Paul, George, and Ringo.

Lest you suppose that crowd following is exclusively a youthful weakness, I should remind you how parents lined up for hours at department stores during the Christmas 1983 shopping season to buy Cabbage Patch dolls for their children. What made this particular mania so curious was that the manufacturer designed the dolls to be ugly. People vying for the limited supply of dolls pushed, scratched, and bit each other, and one woman reportedly suffered a broken leg. Many yielded to the hysteria:

MAILMAN FLIES TO LONDON TO BUY FIVE DOLLS. London (UPI)— A Kansas City mailman left for home yesterday after a $900, four-hour stop in London to pick up five Cabbage Patch dolls he could not get at home.

Edward Pennington, 44, said he came to Britain because his 5-year-old daughter, Leana, was "almost in tears" when Kansas City stores ran out of the dolls—the current rage of the American Christmas shopping season.

Supplies of the British-made versions of the doll were available in major London stores, although Britons were snapping them up as soon as they hit the shelves.

Pennington said he took $900 from his savings to spend four hours in London on his quest. . . . "[A] lot of my neighbors thought I was crazy to make the trip and spend all this money," he said at Heathrow. "But I was determined to get Leana a doll for Christmas."[1]

When people get caught up in a crowd, they stop thinking rationally and allow themselves to be governed almost entirely by emotion. This state of mind prevails at nearly all important market peaks and bottoms. Almost everyone (unanimity) is convinced that the market will keep going up—or down—with no end in sight (hysteria).

During these moments of mass delusion, the crowd extrapolates the current trend too far into the future. The long-term component of market prices becomes grossly (irrationally) exaggerated as investors forget the homely truth that human knowledge has limits, that the future is always uncertain, and that there is no "sure thing" in the economy or the investment markets.

Beware the Consensus

Unfortunately, the market never accommodates a crowd for long. It can't. If the market did what virtually everyone expected it to do, making money would be easy. As any bruised and scarred veteran of the battle for investment survival will tell you, life doesn't work quite that way. In fact, it is logically *impossible* for the market to follow the path that an overwhelming majority of investors believe it will take.

Investors buy because they expect the market to go up. They sell because they expect the market to go down. But if everyone in the marketplace is looking for prices to go up (a consensus), chances are that everyone who is going to buy has already bought. Who is left to bid prices up?

Likewise, if everyone is counting on the market to go down, everyone who is going to sell has probably already sold. Who is left to knock prices down? A tiny minority of dissenters can turn the market around.

Every uptrend—whether primary, intermediate, or short-term—comes to a halt when the last cheerful buyer has emptied his or her wallet, exhausting the buying pressure in the marketplace. By the same token, every downtrend stops when the last discouraged seller dumps his or her goods, exhausting the selling pressure. If investors are unanimously cheerful or unanimously discouraged, prices can only go in the other direction, just as a ball that is thrown high into the air can only come down, or an inner tube that is held under water can only bob up.

In a free market with millions of participants, you will never find a true consensus—100 percent agreement—about anything. A contrarian looks for important market reversals when the *overwhelming majority* of investors expects the prevailing trend to continue. Typically, the size of the majority will be larger at an intermediate turning point than at a short-term peak or bottom. And the majority will be biggest, loudest, and craziest at a primary turning point—the kind that occurs once every couple of years.

Contrarians do *not* argue that "the majority is always wrong." (This is a common misconception.) The majority is often right, especially

11

about the primary trend, for many months at a time. However, the closer it is to a consensus, the more likely that the majority opinion is badly mistaken. As the late Humphrey Neill, the "Vermont ruminator" who is considered the father of contrary investing, used to say: "When everybody thinks alike, everybody is likely to be wrong." A virtually unanimous, emotionally charged majority is almost certain to be wrong.

The Limits of Contrary Thinking

Contrary thinking isn't a cure-all or a get-rich-quick scheme. Like any investment technique, it is an art—not a science. In other words, you must exercise judgment and common sense if you hope to profit from the insights of contrary opinion. Being contrary doesn't relieve you from the obligation of thinking!

Since there is never a perfect consensus in a free market, a contrary investor may sometimes buy or sell too early, at what seems to be a primary turning point, but actually turns out to be an intermediate bottom or top. The primary trend was merely interrupted, not broken. For example, the mood of the gold market was extremely bleak in December 1981 and March 1982. At both points, gold appeared ripe for buying from a contrarian viewpoint. But in each case, the lows turned out to be temporary. After a rally, the market resumed its downtrend and didn't hit a firm bottom until June 1982.

Even the most experienced contrarian will occasionally buy a stock before all the bad news about the company has come out and the stock has hit a true primary bottom. Boston's Batterymarch Financial Management, which shepherds $12 billion of pension fund assets, purchased a large block of Braniff stock just hours before the airline filed for bankruptcy. Yet Batterymarch is one of the most successful pension fund managers in the country, having beaten the market averages every year (with only four exceptions) since 1970.

It is also possible for a contrary investor to sell too early, before the frenzy of the crowd reaches its true peak. In fact, since contrary thinkers are so deeply suspicious of fads, a contrarian may be more inclined than other investors to "pull the trigger" and sell out early when the excitement of a bull market becomes psychologically unbearable.

Contrary thinking, in short, is a *supplement* to—not a *substitute* for—sound fundamental analysis of the economy and the investment markets. Ultimately, the economic laws of supply and demand determine the price of everything, from stocks and gold to the vegetables in your local supermarket. The price of a stock goes up or down with the earnings prospects of a company and the value of its assets. Interest rates fluctuate in response to credit demand and the money supply. Gold tends to move in line with inflation. And so on. To ignore these economic fundamentals is like walking on one leg.

The problem with fundamental analysis, however, is that too often forecasters succumb to the fatal temptation to assume that the future will be just like the recent past. Indeed, the economics profession in the United States has made itself a laughingstock because, at every major turning point for the economy, a host of prominent forecasters manages to predict the opposite of what actually happens.

On Wall Street, analysts face powerful emotional pressure to recommend stocks that have been performing strongly, even after prices have been bid up to untenable levels. Invariably, just before a high-flying stock collapses, many of the best-known Wall Street analysts will be predicting strong earnings gains for the company into the distant future.

These forecasting lapses don't negate the value of fundamental analysis. Rather, they demonstrate that, when you make your forecasts, you need to study the mood of the market *as well as* the economic and financial factors that influence prices. Successful investors can never allow themselves to be married to any widely accepted, pat scenario. They must look for the hidden, potential surprise factors that other forecasters are ignoring. And they must be prepared to change their own forecasts promptly if they see that too many people are adopting their point of view.

Some analysts—the technicians or chartists—maintain that they can predict market movements without any reference to fundamentals. Forget earnings. Forget inflation. Forget the federal deficit. Taking their cue from the academic theoreticians of the efficient market, these gurus maintain that the market price takes into account all the fundamentals, or as one leading stock market technician puts it: "The tape tells all."

Technicians generally look for certain recurring patterns on their price charts: support and resistance levels, head-and-shoulders formations, pennants, double and triple bottoms (or tops), ascending or descending channels, and so on. These patterns are supposed to signal important buying or selling opportunities. Unfortunately, a barrage of computer studies has concluded that the technician's chart patterns are nothing more than optical illusions.

13

Not all technical analysis is voodoo, however, as I demonstrate in Chapter 5. In fact, some of the most reliable technical tools are actually based on contrary thinking. By combining technical analysis with contrary opinion, you can spot trend reversals long before most of the chart readers and thus snap up a much larger share of the profits from any major market move.

The genius of contrary thinking is that it helps you lean the right way at critical market turning points, when emotions drown out reason and other analytical techniques seem to fail. Fundamental analysis and technical analysis tacitly assume that markets are rational. But the markets are *not* rational, at least not always, because people aren't always rational. At the irrational moments, when the lunatics are running the asylum, the contrary investor finds the best opportunities for profit.

2
The Making of a Mania

The only thing we learn from history is that we learn nothing from history.
        —Heinrich Heine

I can calculate the motions of heavenly bodies, but not the madness of people.
        —Sir Isaac Newton

In the spring of 1983, Wall Street was riding a technology boom. High tech stocks were "hot." Although there were hundreds of spectacular gainers, one of the most amazing was Coleco Industries, a company that had made its reputation primarily as a manufacturer of children's plastic swimming pools. Coleco brought out a couple of low-priced computerized video games and a home computer called Adam. Almost overnight, the company was transformed into a high tech sensation.

Coleco stock had been wallowing around $7 a share in August 1982, before the great 1982–83 market surge began. Ten months later, in June 1983, Coleco shares were trading at $65 per share, an incredible 863 percent profit for the handful of investors who were lucky enough to buy at the bottom and sell at the top.

The ride down was even faster, though perhaps not as thrilling unless you were selling the stock short or buying put options to profit from a decline. Coleco shares plunged more than 50 percent from June to August 1983 as the company's earnings from its highly touted computer ventures began to melt away. But the worst was yet to come. By March 1984, only nine months after the high, Coleco stock had nosedived to $10.12 per share—a loss of 84 percent.

Hundreds of other small technology companies (and some not so small) repeated the Coleco story with only slightly less dramatic results.

15

Apple Computer soared five times, then lost 73 percent of its value. Comdisco leaped from a 1982 low of 6¾ to a 1983 high of 42 and promptly collapsed all the way back to 9⅝ by February 1984, a 77 percent loss. The two leading companies in solar-heating technology, A. T. Bliss and American Solar King, both lost approximately 90 percent of their market value between January 1983 and June 1984, after skyrocketing in the first phase of the bull market.

The Boom-Bust Cycle

Was the high tech mania of 1982–83 an isolated incident—a historical freak? Hardly. The same sequence of boom and bust has occurred over and over again in every investment market throughout the world for centuries. Americans are most familiar with the crash of 1929, which followed an orgy of stock speculation. But at least seven notable, though less severe, panics took place in the United States *before* the great crash: in 1819, 1837, 1857, 1873, 1883, 1893, and 1907. A speculative boom in stocks, real estate, gold, or railroad building preceded each collapse.

In retrospect, it is easy to fault our grandfathers for buying stocks at the top of the 1929 boom. But how many of us made the same error in the spring of 1983? Hundreds of thousands of investors eagerly snapped up high tech stocks. Every broker was touting them, and technology mutual funds were springing up everywhere. How many of us bought gold in 1980 when it soared to $600, $700, or $800 an ounce—or silver at $30, $40, or $50 an ounce? Our ancestors had no thicker skulls than we have.

A runaway market distorts investors' senses of value. People begin to believe that prices can only keep going up, up, up, and that anybody with a buck to spare can get rich quickly by playing the market. Driven by greed, the masses forget risk and think only of reward. Yet, for most people, such hysteria is an aberration, not a normal state of mind. Most of the time, most people are fairly sensible and cautious, skeptical of pie-in-the-sky schemes. It is reasonable, therefore, to ask how thousands, even millions of investors can fail to sense that a crash is coming. Why do only a few mavericks recognize that the emperor isn't wearing any clothes?

The answer comes from the venerable Austrian school of economics, whose greatest spokesman in this century was Ludwig von Mises (1881–1973). In his masterpiece, *Human Action*,[1] Mises demonstrated that

16

governments and their servants, the commercial banks, cause the unending boom-and-bust cycles in the economy by expanding artificially the supply of money and credit. When the government (in America, the Federal Reserve) pumps new money into the economy, interest rates drop—at first, anyway. Businesses take out bank loans to finance capital projects that weren't economical at the old, higher interest rates set by the free market. As businesses hire workers and buy equipment and raw materials to carry out their investment plans, the economy picks up and the boom phase of the cycle begins.

But the boom is based on an illusion. The government *appeared* to enlarge the pool of savings available for businesses to invest but it performed this "miracle" by creating money out of thin air. (The government can't create real wealth or real savings, any more than it can turn stones to bread. It can only confiscate wealth through taxation or inflation.) When the government inflates the money supply to reduce interest rates, it in effect steals part of your wealth and lends your money to borrowers at a below-market rate.

This interest subsidy sends a false signal to businesses, encouraging them to invest in projects that the consumer isn't willing to pay for. As the government injects more "funny money" into the economy, the boom heats up. In the business sector, a swelling tide of imprudent investments bids up wages and prices. Finally, to prevent inflation from spinning out of control, the government cuts the flow of credit to businesses and consumers alike, raises interest rates, and precipitates a recession or crash. The crash exposes all the mistaken investments that businesses made during the easy-money period.

Politicians love to expand credit because, if they play their cards correctly, the resulting prosperity (though temporary) will warm the voters' hearts around election time.* Only a killjoy could vote against a man who promised, as Herbert Hoover did in 1928, "a chicken in every pot and a car in every garage." Hoover was swept into office on the strength of one of the greatest credit-induced booms in American history.

---

*Government manipulation of the business cycle is as old as paper money. An insightful book about the phenomenon is Prof. Edward Tufte's *Political Control of the Economy*, Princeton University Press, Princeton, N.J., 1978. Tufte quotes Lord Brougham, a British peer, who complained back in 1814: "A Government is not supported a hundredth part so much by the constant, uniform, quiet prosperity of the country as by those damned spurts which [Prime Minister William] Pitt used to have just in the nick of time." (p. 3.)

Likewise, bankers—who do the government's dirty work by making the loans that puff up the money supply—reap fabulous profits from a credit expansion, at least in the early stages. (Later on, inflation drives up overhead costs and pinches the banks' profit margins.) For a time, investors also make big money from the artificial boom. Typically, the stock market soars in the early phases of a credit expansion. Then, as the inflationary impact of the government's easy-money policy becomes visible, speculation picks up in commodities, real estate, and other tangible assets.

In the end, however, everyone gets burned (even the politicians, if they allow inflation to rage unchecked). During the inevitable down phase of the cycle, businesses must liquidate their unwise investments at a loss. Bankers must write off bad loans that seemed solid just a short time before.

Unwary investors, too, must take their lumps. Stocks, real estate, gold, everything that rocketed sky-high during the boom, plunges back to earth. The crash is unavoidable because the boom fostered an *illusion of value*. Deceived by the government's cheap-credit policy, investors paid far more for their growth stocks, their farmland, their diamonds, coins, and Persian rugs than the long-term prospects for these items justified. When reality caught up, prices came down.

Every speculative mania of the past 300 years (and by extension, every market crash) has resulted from a credit expansion encouraged and, in some cases, directed by the state. When the government injects fiat money into the economy, it upsets the normal balance between savers and borrowers and spurs people to act against their own better judgment, expressed in the market rate of interest before the government began to meddle. If the government rewards people for behaving irrationally, is it any wonder that they accept the invitation?

Charles Mackay, a nineteenth-century Englishman, analyzed three of the earliest known financial manias—the Dutch tulip mania, the Mississippi Company, and the South Sea Bubble—in his classic book, *Extraordinary Popular Delusions and the Madness of Crowds*. Published in 1841, Mackay's book also reviews such nonfinancial fads and follies as alchemy, astrology, haunted houses, witchcraft hysteria, and popular adulation of criminals. This volume belongs on every serious contrarian's bookshelf. After the 1929 stock market crash, financial wizard Bernard Baruch said of Mackay's work: "This book has saved me millions of dollars."

Although Mackay was more interested in the psychological symp-

18

toms of a mania than its economic causes, each of the booms he dis-
cusses began with a credit expansion engineered by the banks, and at
least tacitly supported by the government. For a contrarian, the script
that these old-time manias followed reads like a page out of today's
newspaper.

The Dutch Tulip Mania

The first great financial blowoff of modern times was the Dutch tulip
mania of 1634 to 1636. Tulips were introduced into Europe from Turkey
in the mid-1500s and soon became a status symbol of the wealthy in
Germany and Holland. By 1634, however, Mackay tells us, the rage for
possessing them had spread to the middle classes, "and merchants and
shopkeepers, even of moderate means, began to vie with each other in
the rarity of these flowers and the preposterous prices they paid for
them."[2]

As the mania approached its climax in 1636, regular markets for
rare tulips were established on the Amsterdam Stock Exchange and in
Rotterdam, Haarlem, and other major towns. (When stockbrokers begin
hustling investments they know nothing about—like tulips or, in recent
years, gold and variable annuities—a crash is almost certainly coming.)
A single tulip bulb fetched the incredible price of 6000 Dutch florins,
or about $22,000 in today's money.

"Many people grew suddenly rich," Mackay relates. "A golden bait
hung temptingly out before the people, and one after the other, they
rushed to the tulip-marts, like flies around a honey-pot."[3] The dream
of instant riches enticed the hapless public into the speculation—a
fateful signal that the market was peaking.

Normally, individual investors who buy for cash and hold for the
long term tend to be astute judges of value. But when the public attempts
to speculate—to make the fast buck—it nearly always guesses wrong.
Mackay reports that "nobles, citizens, farmers, mechanics, seamen,
footmen, maid-servants, even chimney-sweeps and old clotheswomen,
dabbled in tulips."[4] Some people sold their houses and lands, or mortgaged them to the banks, just to acquire a collection of bulbs.

Greed shortened everyone's perspective. "Rich people no longer
bought the flowers to keep them in their gardens, but to sell them again
at cent [100] percent profit."[5] Like the California real estate speculators
of the late 1970s who bought single-family homes, not to live in but to

19

sell at a profit a few months later, the tulip traders told themselves that prices could only rise. A futures market for tulips even sprang up, with sellers agreeing to deliver, say, ten tulip bulbs six weeks after the signing of the contract. It was one of the earliest recorded instances of commodity speculation.

Like every speculative mania since, the tulip craze could never have gone as far as it did without the help of the banks (a private monopoly chartered by the Dutch towns). Banking was a fairly new business to seventeenth-century Holland, but bankers had already discovered how to expand credit—and make big profits—by lending out money that customers had deposited with them for safekeeping.

Inflation resulted, as it usually does under fractional-reserve banking systems.* "The prices of the necessaries of life rose again by degrees," Mackay recounts. "Houses and lands, horses and carriages, and luxuries of every sort rose in value with them."[6]

Finally, the whole rotten, credit-crazy structure collapsed. "The more prudent began to see that this folly could not last forever," Mackay says. "It was seen that somebody must lose fearfully in the end. As this conviction spread, prices fell and never rose again."[7] The market value of the once-prized *semper augustus* tulip bulb plunged from 6000 florins to 500 florins—a 91 percent drop. Curiously enough, nearly all of the major financial busts since the seventeenth century have produced losses on a similar scale of 85 to 95 percent.

After prices collapsed, lawsuits broke all over Holland as sellers tried to enforce their tulip-futures contracts. But the judges decided that the contracts were gambling debts, and hence unenforceable at law. Those who owned tulips were stuck with them. Mackay writes the mournful epitaph:

> Many who, for a brief season, had emerged from the humbler walks of life, were cast back into their original obscurity. Substantial merchants were reduced almost to beggary, and many a representative of a noble line saw the fortunes of his house ruined beyond redemption.[8]

---

*Under a fractional-reserve system, banks are allowed to lend out all but a small fraction of their deposits. The minuscule "reserve" that they keep on hand is supposed to cover any withdrawals. Prof. Murray N. Rothbard explains the inflationary impact of fractional-reserve banking in his book, *The Mystery of Banking*, Richardson & Snyder, New York, 1983.

The Mississippi Madness

Nearly a century after the Dutch tulip mania, fiat money sparked a roaring speculative boom in France. The mastermind of the French fiasco was John Law, a flirtatious Scotsman who had fled to the Continent after killing his ladyfriend's lover in a duel. A compulsive gambler, Law was ideally equipped to launch one of history's most egregious flim-flams, the Mississippi Company.

In 1716, Law persuaded the French regent (who was ruling in place of the 6-year-old Louis XV) to allow him to set up a bank. At the time, France was deep in debt and the government had just devalued the coinage, reducing its gold and silver content. Law started out on the right foot. His bank issued paper money fully backed by precious metals, and—unlike the government—Law promised never to change the amount of metal standing behind each note. In fact, he declared that a banker deserved death if he issued notes without enough gold and silver on hand to make redemptions.

French citizens beat a path to his door. Within a year, Law's paper money was trading at a 15 percent premium to the government's coinage. Meanwhile, the government's unbacked paper currency, the *billets d'état* issued during the reign of Louis XIV, had fallen to an 80 percent discount from their nominal value in gold and silver.

Unfortunately, Law's gambling instinct got the better of him. At the regent's urging, he converted his bank into a royal (government) institution. With the blessing of the state, Law began to crank out vast quantities of paper money with no backing whatsoever. Interest rates fell and business picked up. An artificial inflationary boom was under way.

Law quickly hit upon a scheme to exploit the speculative atmosphere he had created. In 1717, the crown granted his Mississippi Company the exclusive right to trade up and down the Mississippi River, including the province of Louisiana, which belonged at the time to France. To attract buyers for the Mississippi Company's stock, Law promised a yearly dividend of 40 percent—an incredible return by the standards of any era.

But Law went a step further. As a favor to his patron who was trying to reduce the national debt, Law told investors they could pay for their subscriptions with the government's next-to-worthless *billets d'état*. Since the dividend was to be paid in real money (gold or silver coin),

Law was in effect promising that shareholders could earn a 120 percent annual yield on their investment from dividends alone.

"The public enthusiasm," Mackay writes, "which had been so long rising, could not resist a vision so splendid."[9] Dukes, marquis, and counts—together with their wives—besieged Law with applications to buy shares. Each new issue was a sellout, even after Law upped the price tenfold! The rue de Quincampoix in Paris, where the great man had his office, was jammed with speculators buying and selling Mississippi Company shares.

As the trading reached a fever pitch, share prices sometimes rose 10 to 20 percent in a few hours—a scene reminiscent of the last days of the 1929 stock market boom. Maids and footmen parlayed their meager savings into instant fortunes. Mackay relates that "many persons in the humbler walks of life, who had risen poor in the morning, went to bed in affluence."[10]

Fueled by fiat money, the artificial boom spread from the rue de Quincampoix across Paris and into the hinterlands. Inflation ran wild, with prices spiraling 300 percent in the space of a few months. Luxury goods rose especially fast as successful speculators channeled their profits into hard assets:

> The looms of the country worked with unusual activity to supply rich laces, silks, broad-cloth and velvets, which being paid for in abundant paper, increased in price fourfold. . . . New houses were built in every direction; an *illusory prosperity* [my emphasis] shone over the land, and so dazzled the eyes of the whole nation, that none could see the dark cloud on the horizon announcing the storm that was too rapidly approaching.[11]

Early in 1720, the first cracks began to appear in Law's magnificent structure. A leading nobleman, the prince de Conti, caused a stir when he brought three wagons full of paper money to Law's bank and demanded payment in specie (metal). The regent browbeat the prince into returning two-thirds of his withdrawal to the bank, but the con game was up. (Fractional-reserve banking is, quite literally, a confidence game. When public confidence evaporates, prompting a rash of withdrawals, the bank fails.) Aware that the banknotes were losing their purchasing power daily, people hurried to cash them in for gold and silver.

However, there wasn't enough specie in Law's bank to satisfy the demand. A run on the bank ensued, together with a disastrous collapse in the price of Mississippi Company stock. Although the government tried to restore confidence in the currency by devaluing gold and silver in terms of paper money, nobody fell for the ruse. The panic only intensified. As a final expedient, the tyrannical regent (like his American counterpart in 1933) forbade private citizens to possess more than a token amount of gold and silver.

In a last-ditch effort to prop up the Mississippi Company's stock, Law asked the government to conscript 6000 Parisian street urchins to work the supposedly abundant gold mines in Louisiana. Law paraded these derelicts through Paris with picks and shovels, convincing a few naive investors that his scheme still had merit.

The price of the stock took a brief bounce—hope springs eternal—but then, as the effects of Law's public-relations stunt wore off, quotations began to slide once more. Mississippi Company shares, which had soared from 500 livres apiece in 1716 to 20,000 livres at the peak in 1720, plunged within a few months to only 200 livres, a staggering 99 percent loss. Law was ruined, and so—very nearly—was the French economy.

The South Sea Bubble

Another famous speculative mania, the South Sea Bubble, took place in 1720 on the other side of the English Channel. Robert Harley, the Earl of Oxford, had founded the South Sea Company in 1711. The new company invited holders of £9 million worth of British government bonds to exchange their bonds for stock in the South Sea Company. For this patriotic service in retiring part of the national debt, the crown granted the South Sea Company a monopoly on British trade with the South Sea islands and South America.

As it turned out, the monopoly wasn't worth anywhere near as much as the earl had dreamed, because Spain, which ruled most of South America at the time, was unwilling to open its colonies to more than a trivial volume of British trade. But like all skillful corporate con artists before and since, Harley knew how to sell an enticing story to a gullible and greedy public. In 1720, the South Sea Company made Parliament an offer it couldn't refuse: the company would absorb virtually the entire national debt of £31 million by issuing South Sea stock to the bondholders.

Robert Walpole, later Britain's first prime minister, denounced the plan in the House of Commons, saying it was designed "to raise artificially the price of the stock, by exciting and keeping up a general infatuation, and by promising dividends out of funds which could never be adequate to the purpose."[12] But Walpole's eloquence was powerless against the earl of Oxford's rumor mill.

The earl's allies whispered that England and Spain were negotiating treaties that would concede to the English free trade with all the Spanish colonies. Gold and silver from the New World would flood into England, making the South Sea merchants the richest on earth. Every hundred pounds invested would return hundreds annually to the stockholder.

The bill passed, and the speculation began. From a price of £128½ per share in January 1720, South Sea stock zoomed to a dizzying £1000 in August. Even Robert Walpole, who had spoken out against the scheme, couldn't resist. He, too, purchased a block of shares (and later lost heavily in the crash). People of all sorts and conditions joined the mad rush to get aboard the bull market.

> It seemed at that time as if the whole nation had turned stock-jobbers [traders]. Exchange Alley was every day blocked up by crowds, and Cornhill [a street in London's financial district] was impassable for the number of carriages. Every body came to purchase stock.[13]

The Bernie Cornfelds of the eighteenth century sensed an opportunity. Noticing how rapidly South Sea Company's shares were running up, swindlers formed hundreds of "bubble companies" that had little or no business purpose other than to peddle their own stock. One company was set up "for trading in hair." Another, which was trying to raise £1 million when it was outlawed, proposed to manufacture a perpetual-motion machine. A third was established "for the transmutation of quicksilver into a malleable fine metal." Since quicksilver, or mercury, is a liquid at any temperature above $-38°$ Fahrenheit, turning it into a solid metal would have been quite an accomplishment.

Perhaps the most remarkable scam was a company with no stated purpose at all. The prospectus coyly hinted that the company had been organized "for carrying on an undertaking of great advantage, but nobody to know what it is."[14] For every £2 invested, the promoter declared that subscribers would be entitled to £100 a year in dividends—a 50 to 1 return. Dazzled by this unsubstantiated promise, a throng of people showed up at the entrepreneur's door the morning after the offering circular was published. In six hours, he collected £2000.

Having raked in a tidy sum for a day's work, the promoter, Mackay says, "was philosopher enough to be contented with his venture, and set off the same evening for the Continent. He was never heard of again."[15]

Of course, we know that today the Securities and Exchange Commission (SEC) would prevent such shady outfits from selling stock to the public. Right? At the height of the new-issues craze in June 1983, a twentieth-century bubble company announced on the front page of its prospectus, which was filed with the SEC:

This offering is of securities of a start-up company with no operating history and *no plan of operation*; the company will not engage in any business whatever until after the completion of this offering. [Emphasis added.]

On page 5, the prospectus further revealed: "The company *does not know what business it will engage in*, has no plan of operation. . . . [my emphasis]"[16] The wording bears a striking resemblance to the advertisement for the bubble company of 1720: "an undertaking of great advantage, but nobody to know what it is." Yet, amazingly, this modern bubble raised $3 million, at $5 per share. Two-and-a-half centuries later, a sucker is still being born every minute.

The South Sea Bubble finally burst in August 1720, when news leaked out that the directors of the company—including the chairman, Sir John Blunt—had sold their stock. This vote of no confidence by the corporate insiders triggered a wave of panic selling that eventually drove the price of South Sea shares from £1000 at the peak to a low of only £135—an 87 percent decline. Thousands of English families were devastated financially, including many members of Parliament, and a general commercial depression settled over the land.

Unsound banking practices, the common denominator of all financial manias, made a scandal like the South Sea Bubble not only possible but inevitable. In Britain, both the quasi-public Bank of England and the private London goldsmiths acted as bankers, making loans to businesses (and later, to stock speculators). In most cases, when a bank made a loan, it issued a note (banknote) secured by the gold and silver in the bank's vaults. Supposedly, the bearer could redeem these banknotes, which circulated as money, in precious metal on demand.

25

However, the Bank of England and the goldsmiths issued far too many notes for the metal they had in storage. This inflationary expansion of credit sparked a huge burst of deceptive "prosperity" from 1715 onward, culminating in the wild stock market boom of 1720. When the crash came, the Bank of England shamefully reneged on its promise to redeem its notes in specie, and many of the goldsmiths went bankrupt.

The Crash of '29

The cycle of financial booms and busts has been repeated throughout the twentieth century, right up to our own times. For Americans, however, the 1929 crash stands out as the granddaddy, the *ne plus ultra*. Enshrined in our national folklore of the Great Depression is the memory of stockbrokers jumping out of windows and former corporate executives selling apples on street corners. More than half a century later, hearts on Wall Street still melt and investors' pulses pound whenever a respected analyst draws a parallel to 1929.

Like the early financial manias described by Mackay in his classic book, the frenetic stock market boom of the late 1920s began with an injection of artificially cheap credit into the economy. In the spring of 1927, the Bank of England lowered interest rates in an attempt to stimulate British industry, which had never really recovered from the World War. As a result of the bank's inflationary policy, gold began to flow out of Britain and into the United States and France. To stem the outflow, Montagu Norman, governor of the Bank of England, persuaded the Federal Reserve to lower interest rates in the United States, spreading the inflation across the Atlantic.

As Federal Reserve governor Adolph C. Miller later complained, it was "the greatest and boldest operation ever undertaken by the Federal Reserve System, and . . . resulted in one of the most costly errors committed by it or any other banking system in the past 75 years."[17] Stock prices exploded in a frenzy of speculation that carried the Dow Jones industrial average from a low of 153 in 1927 to the manic peak of 381 in October 1929—a 149 percent gain in two years. Many individual stocks performed even more spectacularly. Radio Corp., ancestor of today's RCA and a "high tech" stock at the time, gained 500 percent in 1928 alone.

The great innovation of the 1927–29 stock market boom was leverage. Margin accounts mushroomed as speculators borrowed money from their brokers at low interest rates to buy common stocks. (*Margin* is Wall Street jargon for the deposit or down payment you must make when you borrow money from your broker to finance securities purchases.) In early 1928, it was possible to take out a margin loan at only 5 percent interest.

Even after margin rates rose sharply—to 12 percent in late 1928 and a peak of 20 percent in March 1929—speculators eagerly incurred huge debts to buy high-flying stocks. When the crash came, brokers demanded that their customers put up more collateral to support these shaky loans. Rather than meet the broker's "margin call," overextended speculators dumped their shares on the market, forcing prices down even further.

Hundreds of closed-end investment companies were formed during the late 1920s. These companies, whose purpose was to invest in the stocks of other companies, issued their own shares, which traded on the exchanges. Some of these early closed-end funds still survive. Most, however, came to grief during the crash because they had borrowed heavily (usually by issuing bonds or preferred stock) to buy common stocks during the boom. Some 160 funds existed at the beginning of 1927; 140 were formed that year, 186 in 1928, and an astonishing 265 in 1929. The magic of leverage was irresistible.

As the boom approached its zenith, the promise of instant riches sucked thousands of amateurs into the market. Some made fortunes, lending credibility to the myth of wealth without work:

The rich man's chauffeur drove with his ears laid back to catch the news of an impending move in Bethlehem Steel; he held 50 shares himself on 20-point margin. The window-cleaner at the broker's office paused to watch the ticker, for he was thinking of converting his laborious accumulated savings into a few shares of Simmons. Edwin Lefevre (an articulate reporter on the market at this time who could claim considerable personal experience) told of a broker's valet who made nearly a quarter of a million in the market, of a trained nurse who cleaned up thirty thousand following tips given her by grateful patients; and of a Wyoming cattleman, 30 miles from the nearest railroad, who bought or sold a thousand shares a day.[18]

The market was bursting with extravagant optimism, the epitome being the famous comment by Prof. Irving Fisher of Yale (himself a director of an investment company) several weeks before the crash: "Stock prices have reached what looks like a permanently high plateau."[19] Not everyone agreed, of course. *Poor's Weekly Business and Investment Letter* warned of "the great common-stock delusion" and William P. Hamilton, editor of the *Wall Street Journal*, had a premonition of the end when he wrote his historic editorial, "A Turn of the Tide," on October 25, 1929. But the great majority of investors and pundits shared ex-President Coolidge's faith, reiterated just before he left office in March 1929, that the economy was "absolutely sound" and that stocks were "cheap at current prices."[20]

From the manic top of October 1929 to the panic bottom of July 1932, the Dow industrials plummeted 89 percent—an across-the-board wipeout of stock market values, the like of which has never been seen, before or since, in American financial history. Excessive credit expansion had ruined the fortunes of millions of Americans from the stock speculator on Wall Street to the shopkeeper on Main Street.

Can It Happen Again?

As long as governments, working hand-in-glove with the private banking system, continue to inflate the supply of money and credit, speculative manias will recur—followed by gut-wrenching busts. Cheap money gives a false stimulus to the economy. Business executives undertake projects that can never pay off, and investors, duped by the same monetary illusion, throw their hard-earned savings into crackpot ventures that are doomed to failure. A credit-based boom spawns a "cluster of errors," in Prof. Murray Rothbard's words. It distorts people's judgments and induces a kind of mass insanity.

At the beginning of this chapter, I cited the speculative boom in technology stocks that came to a head in the spring of 1983. This mania resulted from a record-breaking monetary expansion engineered by the Federal Reserve from roughly June 1982 to July 1983. In those twelve months ending in July 1983, the basic U.S. money supply grew almost 14 percent, the most rapid expansion in any year since the Federal Reserve was created. (See Chapter 8 for the inflationary implications of this runaway money growth.)

To its credit, the Fed pulled back on the monetary reins from mid-1983 onward. Money growth dipped to 5 percent year-over-year in late 1984, prompting some analysts to worry that the Fed might push the economy into a recession. However, it is wise to recall that in most cycles, money growth *accelerates* as the cycle matures. Hence, the worst monetary abuses of the current cycle may yet lie ahead. If Paul Volcker and his colleagues, under pressure from the White House and Congress, open up the monetary spigots in 1985, the U.S. economy could face a once-in-a-lifetime crisis in which the Federal Reserve and the political authorities will have to choose between allowing a crackup boom (with highly inflationary consequences) or forcing the economy through a deflationary wringer to squeeze out the errors and excesses that have built up as a result of fifty years of credit expansion.

My guess is that the moral and intellectual fiber of this country is too strong to allow hyperinflation. But as the peak of the current credit cycle draws near in 1985 or 1986, another speculative blowoff, perhaps rivaling that of 1983, will likely precede it in stocks, commodities, precious metals, or real estate. The following characteristics, which have signaled every financial mania since the Dutch tulip craze of 1636, will help you recognize the psychology of a boom that is about to bust. When more than two or three of these symptoms appears at once, it is time to sell: The undertaker is at the door.

Nine Symptoms of a Dying Boom

- *A breathtaking, parabolic rise in prices,* accompanied by predictions that the advance will go on indefinitely.

- *A widespread rejection of old standards of value.* According to the apologists for the boom, the dawning of a "new era" makes today's high prices reasonable, even cheap, no matter how outrageous they would have seemed only yesterday. Hustlers take advantage of inflated values to promote lower-quality goods as top-grade merchandise.

- *A proliferation of dubious investment schemes* promising huge returns in an inordinately short time.

- *Intense and—for a time—successful speculation by uninformed members of the public,* fostering the belief that making money in the market is easy, a "sure thing."

- *Popular fascination with leveraged investments,* such as futures, options, or margin accounts, which enable the speculator to control a large block of assets with a small down payment.

- *Heavy selling by corporate "insiders"* and other conservative investors with a long-term orientation.

- *Extremely high trading volume* that enriches brokers and snarls paperwork as back offices try to keep track of the many transactions.

- *Absurd or even violent behavior* by people who are desperately trying to get their hands on the booming asset. (Remember the "grown-ups" who punched and scratched each other to buy a Cabbage Patch doll.)

Three hundred years of booms and busts demonstrate that human nature changes little, if at all, over the centuries. Most investors dream of a fast, easy track to riches. During a credit-induced economic boom, this illusion takes on a sheen of plausibility. The inescapable lesson of history, however, is that wealthbuilding takes time, work, good saving habits, and—perhaps most important—the emotional discipline to steer away from investment fads. When the crowd decides it has found El Dorado, the contrary investor hops aboard the first boat home.

3

I Saw It in the
New York Times

All I know is what I read in the newspapers.
—Will Rogers

Americans have always stood in awe of the printed word. Perhaps this habit of mind goes back to our Puritan ancestors, who were "people of the Book." We couldn't imagine governing ourselves without a written constitution. Whenever we want to make sure someone lives up to a promise, we ask him to "put it in black and white"—a testimony to our faith in the power of print.

Will Rogers was kidding, of course, when he claimed to know nothing except what the newspapers told him. But why do we laugh at his gag? Partly, at least, because it is a caricature of how many people really think. Many people *do* take the preachments of the media as gospel. Not long ago, a public-opinion poll singled out TV newscaster Walter Cronkite as the most trusted figure in America, even though studies have repeatedly charged CBS with blatant political bias in its reporting of the news during Cronkite's tenure.[1] Most people, unfortunately, are quite willing to let someone else analyze and interpret the news for them, rather than do the hard intellectual labor themselves.

The mass media—newspapers, magazines, radio, and TV—dispense a mixture of fact and opinion (or interpretation). As an investor, you must always distinguish between these two elements when you monitor the financial news. Treat facts with reverence. When the Labor Department reports that consumer prices rose at a 4 percent annual rate

31

last month, pay attention. (You can be sure the markets are tuning in.) But if the White House press secretary goes on the air to proclaim that the latest consumer price figures *prove* that inflation has been vanquished and that the president's program is working, he or she is simply expressing an opinion—with perhaps little or no logical basis. In matters of opinion, reserve the right to make up your own mind.

Above all, don't march unthinkingly behind the opinions of any supposed expert, including the author of this book. Ask yourself: Does this line of reasoning make sense to me, or is something missing? What unforeseen events could upset this expert's forecast? The mere fact that the *New York Times* hails Professor Dryasdust as an authority doesn't make his opinions about the future course of the economy or the investment markets any more compelling.

Quite the contrary can be true: financial experts who get written up in the news media nearly always make their most wildly inaccurate prognostications at or close to important market peaks and bottoms. Even the most learned gurus with their Ph.D.s in economics or finance can—and regularly do—fall into the trap of crowd thinking. (Running with the crowd is a psychological, not an intellectual, failing.) By carefully studying the financial pages of your daily newspaper, you can detect an emerging consensus—when everybody is thinking alike. If you go promptly to the opposite side of the market, chances are good that you will emerge with a profit.

Because of their frequent publishing schedule, daily newspapers can help you spot changes in the market's short-term trend, as well as shifts in the intermediate- and long-term trends. My favorite newspaper for reading the mood of the investment markets is actually the *Wall Street Journal*, not the *New York Times*. The *Times* has the most comprehensive financial section of any general-interest daily in the United States, which makes for valuable supplementary reading. But the *Journal* covers many more markets, and in greater detail. If you don't already subscribe to the *Journal*, I recommend that you make the investment— if only for the wealth of misguided professional opinion you will find reported there, dependably, at every significant market peak or bottom.

News magazines like *Time*, *Newsweek*, and *Business Week* can also provide useful contrary insights when they quote the opinions of presumed financial authorities. In particular, cover stories in these magazines often signal that the intermediate- or long-term trend of the economy or the markets is ready to do an about face. Paul Macrae Montgomery, analyst with the brokerage firm of Legg Mason Wood

Walker in Newport News, Virginia, has studied over 3000 *Time* covers going back to 1924—a labor that must have been as pleasant as cleaning the Augean stables. Montgomery found that in four out of five cases where a financial question was treated on the cover of *Time*, the outcome within a year was just the opposite of what the magazine's editors had foreseen.[2]

All of the slick newsweeklies are determined followers of fashion—they know what sells magazines. When they splash a dramatic, emotional message on the front cover, you can safely conclude that they are reflecting the consensus of the crowd. For example, in early October 1983, *Business Week* ran a cover announcing that IBM was "the winner" in its struggle with Apple for dominance in the personal computer market. As it transpired, the victory party was a bit premature. A week later, IBM made its high for the year on the Big Board. Over the next eight months, IBM shares (the bluest of the blue chips) plunged 26 percent—a far worse performance than the Dow Jones industrial average. (Apple, meanwhile, soared 65 percent.) Next winner, please?

In the spring of 1984, a series of hysterical magazine covers suggested that nuclear power had, in the immortal words of *Time*, "bombed out." *Financial World* (June 13) chimed in with a cover story that purported to deliver "a postmortem on the ill-fated nuclear power industry." *Barron's* (June 4), exploiting the gloom of the hour, cast doubt upon not only the nuclear companies but the entire utility industry: "Do Utilities Have a Future?" (In *Barron's* defense, the answer the article gave was a qualified *yes*.) And *Business Week*, which in recent years has adopted a brassy style of journalism that makes it almost as good a contrary indicator as *Time*, asked baldly (May 21): "Are Utilities Obsolete?"

For a contrarian, this long series of articles condemning electric utilities—and nuclear utilities in particular—suggested that the worst was just about over for utility stocks. The darkest fears that anyone could conjure up were already built into the prices of the stocks. Hence, the chances of a favorable surprise were running high. As I wrote at the time in *Personal Finance*, "Utilities are no more 'obsolete' than lightbulbs." The feverish publicity about the problems of the electric power industry, I said, actually amounted to "the strongest buy signal for utility stocks that you're likely to see in your lifetime."

You know the rest. The Dow Jones utility average made its low for 1984 on May 29, just one week after *Business Week* had pronounced the industry "obsolete." Utility stocks skyrocketed for the rest of the

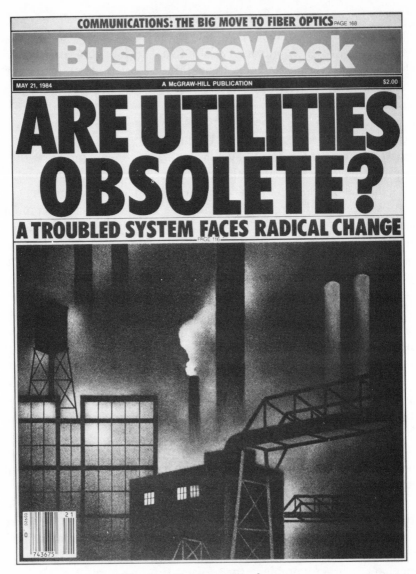

Fig. 1.   *Business Week* cover

year, paced by the companies with heavy nuclear investment. Some nukes leaped 40, 50, or even 100 percent from their yearly lows.

Reading Between the Lines

For precise timing, however, nothing beats your daily newspaper. Regardless of what newspaper you read, and regardless of the market you're interested in, the signs of an approaching reversal are the same. When virtually all the seers quoted in your newspaper say the market is headed up—and some affirm that it is about to skyrocket—prices are due to drop. On the other hand, when the vast majority of commentators say the market is going to keep sinking—and some predict a bloodbath—a rally is imminent.

You will inevitably find unanimity and hysteria, the twin characteristics of a crowd mentality, in the comments of the leading market analysts near important tops and bottoms. In a newspaper roundup of analysts' opinions, however, hysteria is usually more prominent than unanimity—for a good reason.

Any responsible reporter (and most of the people who work for the *Journal* or other leading newspapers are conscientious journalists) will try whenever possible to present all sides of a controversial issue. Since predictions about the investment markets are, like politics and religion, open to controversy, reporters often give disproportionate space to dissenting views.

Don't let one or two vaguely hopeful remarks in a deep bear market, or a couple of mildly cautious remarks in a soaring bull market, throw you off track. Ask yourself: Is the overwhelming preponderance of sentiment on the other side? Contrary investing doesn't require you to go against literally everybody else—just against the great majority. Inevitably, a few dissenters (contrarians, whether they know it or not) will correctly call the turn. Don't scorn them, join them!

At an important stock market bottom, for example, it isn't unusual to discover a few technical analysts who argue that the market is "deeply oversold." Other analysts may admit that stocks look like "great values for the longer term." Typically, though, even the few analysts who haven't been shell-shocked by the bear market are too timid to say: "The bottom is here, buy with both hands." They cloak their bullishness in rhetoric about the virtues of patience and of a long-term perspective. (All very true, of course.) They don't want to be pinned down to a specific timetable for a market recovery.

Likewise, at a peak, a few analysts will wonder aloud how much higher the market can rise without a correction. Some may complain about excessive speculation. But almost nobody says: "Sell now, a crash is coming." In fact, these cautious bears often concede—to be on the safe side—that the market's advance may keep going a while longer.

A Note of Hysteria

Nonetheless, voices of reason are a distinct minority when the market comes under the sway of a strong bullish or bearish consensus. At these critical extremes, a note of hysteria creeps into the thinking of many analysts who normally seem calm and self-possessed. To determine when a crowd has formed, watch for reckless or desperate statements by respected establishment advisers, not the Howard Ruffs or the Jerome Smiths, but the mainstream analysts at the old-line investment firms.

You can always find some maverick prophet somewhere who is willing to predict that almost any market is going to the moon—or through the floor. These predictions may well be hysterical, but *they don't represent the consensus.* A contrarian takes a stand against the overwhelming majority, not against a small fringe element of the investment community.

It would be a mistake, for instance, to take a bullish attitude toward the stock market merely because Joe Granville is bearish. Granville doesn't speak for the mainstream of stock market technicians (not anymore, at least). He has stubbornly urged "Sell all stocks!" for so long that he has lost most of his following. Granville speaks for himself and a handful of perennial bears who still listen to him. His advice is occasionally correct, but only in the sense that a stopped clock occasionally gives the correct time.

By the same token, it would be a misuse of contrary opinion to assert that gold prices are likely to fall because the celebrated Aden sisters of Costa Rica are predicting (even with gold under $350 as I write) that the metal will soar above $2000 an ounce by 1986. To some people, such a prediction—like Jerome Smith's forecast of $200-an-ounce silver within the same period—may seem outlandish and hysterical on the face of it.

I must admit that the idea of $2000 gold and $200 silver also strains the imagination of a "moderate goldbug" like myself. But from a contrarian standpoint, neither Jerome Smith nor the Adens represent a consensus view on gold or silver. Only a small minority of metals investors are basing their plans on these forecasts. Hence, there is nothing to be gained by going contrary to the Adens or Jerome Smith.

36

A diehard's opinions are significant only when he or she capitulates. If, say, Joe Granville suddenly *reversed* his long-standing bearish stance and recommended buying stocks, a contrarian would sit up and take notice. Granville would probably switch to buying stocks only if the psychological pressure from the bulls became irresistible—as it tends to be right at the top!

James Dines, the self-proclaimed "original goldbug," promised his subscribers in 1962 that he would give them one "much vaunted all-out one and only gold and silver sell signal." He chose to give it on June 17, 1982—two trading days before gold made its most recent cyclical bottom. His capitulation was actually a ringing buy signal because it indicated that the last person in the marketplace who could have sold had finally decided to do so. The market had nowhere to go but up.

As colorful as some of the fringe analysts may be, the people whose views you should study if you are trying to gauge the real mood of the marketplace are the analysts and traders at the major banks, brokerage firms, and other financial institutions. These people control (or influence) the deployment of literally trillions of dollars' worth of assets. They wield far more power than Joe Granville, the Aden sisters, or Jerome Smith. *They* represent the mainstream. When these respected blue chip advisers blow their cool, run—don't walk—to the other side of the market!

Most of the time, people who hold responsible positions in the investment establishment shy away from making extravagant forecasts (at least in public). It isn't good for business. People don't generally entrust their money to kooks. As a result, most investment advisers with prestigious credentials tend to be cautious when talking to the press—if they give interviews at all.

At major market turning points, though, a few respected establishment advisers invariably get caught up in the emotions of the mob and "let it all hang out." For a contrarian, the emotionally charged statements of these advisers virtually leap off the newspaper page, shouting "Buy!" (when fear grips the market) and "Sell!" (when euphoria carries the day).

If you suffer from an inferiority complex, you can give your ego a much needed boost by keeping a file of flaky forecasts by normally sensible investment advisers. Even the best and the brightest investment professionals with years of academic training and on-the-job experience can lose their emotional equilibrium when the crowd stampedes. Let's take a look at some of the kinds of comments they make when the market is about to reverse field.

Stock Market Bloopers

The 1973–74 bear market on Wall Street brought the worst collapse of stock prices since the 1929 crash. The Dow Jones industrial average skidded 45 percent and hundreds of other stocks took an even worse pounding. Avon Products, one of the "Nifty Fifty" stocks that every bank, mutual fund, and insurance company wanted to own during the previous bull market, plummeted 87 percent. Polaroid, another crowd favorite, nose-dived an incredible 91 percent.

Most stocks, and most of the major averages, except the Dow industrials, hit bottom in early October 1974. The morning after the market reached its nadir, a battle-hardened veteran analyst with the brokerage firm of Laidlaw-Coggeshall, Inc., was quoted in the *Journal:* "I've been in this business since 1937, and *I don't think I've ever seen a market this bad.* I'd like to see some stabilization . . . but *I've almost given up* on resistance points" [emphasis added].[3]

Worst market in thirty-seven years? Giving up hope for a stabilization (to say nothing of a rally)? This is the mood of despair (or fear) that always envelops the marketplace at a major bottom.

The week before, the investment chief at Marine Midland Bank had suggested the bottom was near when he opined that the market "looks like a screaming buy" but that *"nobody wants to be the first in the water."*[4]* At the bottom, the timid bull sees bargains all around but is too afraid to buy. This type of remark is common at both primary and intermediate market lows. A variant is the statement that "there are no buyers to be found" or "the buyers are on strike." A contrarian who sees such comments can almost hear the ghost of J. Paul Getty thundering, "Buy when everyone else is selling."

In December 1974, the same day the Dow Jones industrials touched their bear market low, a distinguished analyst with Reynolds Securities, who still appears on TV's *Wall Street Week,* told the *Journal:* "Stock market participants are *giving up hope* that the October lows will hold."[5] This gentleman was merely articulating the despair that millions of investors felt—at the exact bottom of the bear market. Similar comments

---

*In the following pages, the emphases added have been my own.

by other pundits appear at the bottom of every bear market, regardless of the type of investment.

More recently, the same mood of fear and despair was rampant in August 1982, just before the stock market launched into its historic ascent. (The Dow industrials gained 61 percent in ten months, the steepest rise in the shortest time since 1932–33.) According to a Tulsa money manager who was quoted in the *Journal* the morning after the Dow bottomed at 777, the fact that the market had "demonstrated no ability to rally on good news [of lower interest rates] probably indicates that a *selling climax* will be required to end the bear market."[6]

A selling climax, also known as a *waterfall decline*, is probably the most dreaded phenomenon in any market. Prices go straight down without interruption. As disheartened investors dump their holdings at any price, trading volume soars.

Simply talking about the possibility of a selling climax is enough to send chills up the typical investor's spine. When prices are making an important low, however, frightened bears will often *predict* a climax—not recognizing that one has just taken place under their noses!

Many analysts seem to think that markets customarily form a bottom after a climactic burst of heavy trading. Just the opposite is true. Bear markets usually end, as T. S. Eliot might have said, "not with a bang but a whimper." The climax that occurs at the end of most declines is really an anticlimax: trading volume drops, selling pressure dries up, and the bear market fades away.

By contrast, heavy volume at the end of a market rise usually indicates a climactic blowoff, a last burst of euphoria that exhausts the buying pressure in the marketplace. Oddly enough, few analysts are willing to acknowledge a buying climax when they see one. Instead, they predict that the heavy trading will push the market even higher. The activity and excitement blind them to the fact that the market is tracing out an important top.

The same day our Tulsa money manager was warning of a selling climax, a vice president of E. F. Hutton & Co. told the *Journal* that investors were witnessing "the most emotional period [of the bear market] with *outright capitulation and panic selling* by both large and small investors."[7] He was right, of course. However, he failed to draw the obvious conclusion: if most investors were capitulating and selling in a panic, it was time to mortgage the kids and buy.

The newspapers, in short, clearly signaled the onset of the powerful bull market that took off in August 1982. If, contrary to what these hysterical commentators were advising, you had bought stocks, you could have made a fortune. But the nicest part of the story is that the respectable pundits don't simply tell you when to buy. They also tip you off when it is time to sell.

At the top of the last bull market for stocks in November 1980, the *Journal* interviewed an analyst who estimated that the Dow industrials would range for the *rest of the decade* between 1000 and 2000.[8] A ten-year bull market! Great expectations, wouldn't you say? Especially since, at the time, the Dow had barely edged over 1000 (on the strength of the Reagan landslide).

Alas, the same week, most stocks on the Big Board slipped into a severe twenty-one-month bear market that shaved 25 percent off the Dow and 31 percent off the broader-based New York Stock Exchange composite index. The starry-eyed bulls who thought the Dow wouldn't go below 1000 for the rest of the decade were ground up into hamburger.

At the top of the huge speculative boom in the spring of 1983, the chairman of a $10 billion investment management firm in Los Angeles told the *Journal*, "I have *never felt more confident* in maintaining a fairly fully invested equity position." Another money manager talked about "the *exciting gains* in store for corporate profits."[9] Those happy-go-lucky opinions were published the morning after most stocks peaked for the year. A few days later, the same analyst who had given up hope in October 1974 (when stocks were cheap) called for "a continuation of the *irrespressible bull market*." "We're in a *new era of investor confidence*," he added.[10] This savant managed to be wrong at both the exact top and the exact bottom of the two most extreme markets in fifty years. As far as I know, he still has his job.

Gold Market Follies

When the stock market is about to make a dramatic turnaround, you can be sure that several esteemed gurus will jump off the deep end— publicly—in your daily newspaper. But contrary thinking is a valid approach to any market, not simply the stock market. Indeed, advisers in the gold and silver markets regularly serve up some of the most delectable morsels that a contrarian will find anywhere.

In mid-January 1980, with gold changing hands at the stratospheric price of $744 an ounce (up from $475 a month earlier), a trader for

Drexel Burnham Lambert told the *Journal* that "the potential to see $1000 gold in the next week is easy," and that he wouldn't be surprised if gold reached $1500 in February.[11] When normally cautious establishment types project a 33 percent gain in *one week* and a 100 percent gain in a month, you can safely deduce that the market has lost its senses. The roof is ready to cave in.

In the same issue of the *Journal*, a London dealer "at a large firm" said he wouldn't be "at all surprised" to see gold at $1000 an ounce. "It's good business," this thoughtful gentleman confided, "but, looked at objectively, it's pretty horrifying. We're all booking our beds in the looney bin."[12] As this comment shows, it is not unusual for sober analysts to recognize, at a speculative peak, that the market has gone mad. Nonetheless, like moths attracted to a flame, they can't bear to take their profits and fly away. Instead, greedy for the last penny of gain, they continue to believe that the market will go up.

The next day's *Journal* (January 18) printed the ultimate hysterical view of the market. Gold had closed on New York's Commodity Exchange the previous afternoon at $802 an ounce. A trader, again from Drexel Burnham as it happens, said: "We're in a *runaway market*. It's almost like going to a strip show knowing the place is about to be raided. *No one wants to leave* until they're sure the party's over"(emphasis added).[13]

That comment appeared in Friday's newspaper. On Monday, the party was over. The price of gold touched an all-time high of $875 on the Comex, then plunged to $825 at the close. A bone-crunching two-and-a-half-year bear market had begun, with gold sinking to $297 by June 1982.

Precious metals seem to excite violent emotions at the bottom of the market as well as at the top. A treasured clipping in my file is a Commodity News Service story that appeared in *Western Mining News* a few days after gold made its most recent primary bottom in June 1982. Headlined "$190 Gold? Analysts Disagree," the article reported that an analyst with ContiCommodity envisioned a "long-term downside objective" of $191 an ounce for gold.[14]

Most of the time, responsible analysts (of gold or any other market) tend to predict that prices will fluctuate in a narrow range. Conventional thinkers prefer to assume that the patterns of the recent past will carry into the future, because that position usually appears to be safe. Conformists know that if they forecast a sharp move up or down, they run the risk of being proved *very* wrong. They might acquire the reputation of being cranks or oddballs—deadly for anyone with ambitions in a big organization.

When the market is trending strongly in one direction, however, the bolder types within the investment community throw caution to the winds and predict that the market will take off like a runaway railroad car *in the direction of the existing trend.* Beware of a respectable mainstream adviser who says the price of gold is going to plunge another 30 percent, after it has already plunged 60 percent in the past two years! This person is thinking with his or her emotions.

Interestingly enough, our analyst from ContiCommodity who was looking for $191 gold based his bearishness on a familiar argument: "There is nothing to indicate the selling has climaxed," he said. The climax, of course, was taking place as he spoke. But he couldn't see it, because he had worked himself into a mood of exaggerated pessimism. "I am waiting for the public to start selling its gold," the Conti analyst maintained. "When John Q. Public decides his Krugerrand is worthless and sells it, that's when I will buy."

This man obviously *thought* he was acting contrary to the majority. But he was waiting for the impossible: John Q. Public will never decide that his Krugerrand is worthless. (In fact, as shown in Chapter 8, the small investor has a good record for buying physical metals near the bottom of the market and selling them near the top.) By refusing to change his mind unless some impossible condition was met, the analyst from ContiCommodity showed that he was really endorsing the prevalent bearish consensus. He wasn't thinking independently at all.

The contrary investor must guard against the fatal temptation to become gloomier and gloomier as prices fall. Instead, train yourself to become increasingly cheerful as prices decline, because you know the market is drawing closer to its ultimate bottom! Likewise, you should feel more and more nervous as prices rise, because the market is approaching its ultimate top. When the risk in the market seems highest (at the bottom), it is really lowest because there is no room left for prices to fall. On the other hand, when the risk seems lowest (at the top), it is really highest because there is no room left for prices to rise.

Telling the Trends Apart

Perhaps the most difficult task facing any investor—but especially those investors who rely on their newspapers for buy and sell signals—is to distinguish the primary from the intermediate trend, and the intermediate from the short-term trend. Investors with a long-term perspective (six months to two years) want to buy as close as possible to a primary bottom and sell as close as possible to a primary top. If they miss the primary turning point, they try to buy at the bottom of an intermediate reaction or sell at an intermediate peak.

Investors with an intermediate time horizon (six weeks to six months) seek to buy at an intermediate low and sell at an intermediate high. But if the intermediate turning point slips by them, they look for the next short-term low at which to buy (or a short-term high at which to sell).

Traders with a short-term viewpoint (less than six weeks) have the hardest job of all. If they miss the turning point, they either must make their move as quickly as possible (taking the risk that the market may reverse on them), or they can stand aside and wait until the next short-term peak or bottom provides another opportunity to trade.

In general, newspaper commentary isn't especially helpful to the short-term trader, because respected investment analysts usually don't lose their nerve at minor turning points. (For the short-term speculator, I describe a number of more sophisticated contrarian trading techniques in later chapters.) However, the more extreme the statements by establishment pundits, the more likely that the market has reached a turning point of longer-term significance.

Near intermediate or primary tops and bottoms, newspapers and magazines often begin to run emotionally tinged feature (background) articles about the market, in addition to the usual daily commentary. For instance, when the gold market was forming an intermediate bottom around $335 an ounce in July and August of 1984, the *Wall Street Journal* and *Barron's* published a flurry of full-length articles pooh-poohing gold.

Barron's carried an interview with investment adviser John Dessauer, titled "Crash in Gold: Analyst Sees Only Short Respite"[15] and another with Harry Schultz, headlined "The Greening of a Gold Bug."[16] On July 9, the same day gold made an important (though not its final) low, the *Journal* ran an interesting feature noting that while most professionals were expecting gold prices to slide further, the average person was buying gold coins heavily. Coin dealers were swamped with retail orders to buy Krugerrands and other bullion coins—a recurring phenomenon at important market bottoms. Small investors who pay cash and buy for the long term typically have a much better sense of value than the professional analysts at the giant brokerage houses. If only the pros had the humility to listen to them!

Of course, there is no guarantee that hysterical newspaper or magazine articles will always coincide precisely with a significant market turning point. Even though contrary opinion is a powerful timing tool, it isn't perfect—no investment technique is. Sometimes contrary thinking will put you into a market a bit early and take you out a bit early, since extremes of crowd psychology don't always coincide precisely with the highest or the lowest price. Over the long pull, though, the connection is amazingly close, as I will explain further in Chapter 4.

Catching the Big One

Fortunately for long-term investors who don't like to trade frequently, primary turning points are usually the easiest to recognize. The dispensers of investment wisdom become irrepressibly hopeful or unrelentingly gloomy. Dramatic predictions abound. Feature articles in newspapers and magazines report on the blessings or disasters that the market has wrought. *Time* or *Newsweek* may even devote a cover story to the market.

At a major cyclical turning point, it isn't uncommon for a book touting or condemning the market to reach the bestseller list. In 1979, for example, Howard J. Ruff's *How to Survive and Prosper During the Coming Bad Years* became the best-selling financial book in history. A close runner-up was my friend Douglas Casey's book, *Crisis Investing*, which hit the bestseller list in September 1980. Both books strongly recommended precious metals as a hedge against the likelihood of accelerating inflation in the 1980s.

In fairness to Casey and Ruff, I should note that neither is a bigoted goldbug and both have urged their followers on various occasions to sell (as well as buy) precious metals. Nonetheless, it was hardly an accident that their books captured the mass imagination just when metals prices were exploding—before a devastating collapse. In retrospect, the successes of the Casey and Ruff books should have warned the contrary investor that precious metals and other inflation hedges were nearing a primary peak.

Scoffers who, with 20-20 hindsight, smirk at the Casey and Ruff books should recall that one of the most talked-about financial books of 1983 (although it didn't make the bestseller list) was titled *Is Inflation Ending? Are You Ready?* by A. Gary Shilling and Kiril Sokoloff. The U.S. inflation rate hit a cyclical bottom in July 1983, a few months after the Shilling/Sokoloff tome came off the press.

Moreover, as you would expect, extreme and emotional forecasts for inflation by leading economists accompanied the most recent cyclical lows. Arnold X. Moskowitz, chief economist at Dean Witter Reynolds, takes the prize for the most preposterous comment: "Inflation is going down to zero—permanently."[17] He was wrong before he reached the second half of the sentence. As late as the summer of 1984, more than a year after consumer prices had begun to rise more swiftly again, respected pundits were still writing obituaries for inflation. In its August 20, 1984, issue, for example, *Business Week* published an article that proclaimed hopefully: "Zero Inflation: An Impossible Dream That May Come True."

For a contrarian, it is almost impossible *not* to conclude that the U.S. inflation rate made a major bottom in the summer of 1983, commemorated by a book that was perfectly suited to the occasion. Perhaps the next round of price increases won't be as severe as what the nation suffered under Nixon and Carter. Perhaps, in a long-term sense, the inflation rate is "coming down the other side of the mountain," from the 15 percent peak in 1980. But, given what Shilling and the other worthies have told us, it is likely that—at least in 1985 and 1986—prices will rise faster than most observers currently expect.

Naturally, a book isn't published at every primary turning point to warn you that the market is about to shift gears. Often, you must rely on an accumulation of signals from newspapers, magazines, TV, and other media to know when a change in the primary trend is at hand. Interpreting these signals is an art, not a science. As a rule, though, the more frightened you feel when you decide to go against the crowd, the more likely that the market is presenting you with a major buying or selling opportunity.

In addition, as you will see in the next few chapters, there are many

45

statistical indicators you can track to confirm the message from the news media. These indicators give you objective evidence of what investors in the marketplace are thinking. But since even the best of statistical indicators can occasionally go haywire, you should never overlook the indicator that is sitting on your doorstep every morning. All you really need to know is right there, in black and white.

4
Roll Out the Polls

If 40 million people say a foolish thing, if does not become a wise one.

—W. Somerset Maugham

Newspapers, magazines, and books will usually give you a pretty good idea of the market's mood. But sophisticated contrarians rely on a bevy of statistical indicators to help read the mind of the crowd more precisely. One of the easiest—and most accurate—ways to determine whether the market is approaching unanimous agreement (hence, a reversal) is by taking a poll.

Ideally, a pollster who wanted to gauge the mood of the market could collect a scientific sampling of several thousand investors nationwide (or worldwide) and ask them whether they thought prices were headed up or down. However, since markets fluctuate so quickly, altering the lineup of bulls and bears, it would be necessary to take a poll weekly, or even more frequently, to keep the data fresh. So far, nobody has attempted such a costly project, although someday videotext technology may make it possible for thousands, or even millions, of investors to register their opinions of the market at regular intervals on a central computer.

The next best thing to polling the investors themselves is a survey of investment advisers. In fact, since investment advisers tend to shape the thinking of their clients, this elite group may provide an even better insight into the market's likely direction. Certainly, it isn't difficult to find out what investment advisers are thinking. They publish hundreds of newsletters laying out their opinions for all to see. Careful readers who have subscribed to a newsletter for a while can readily judge from the author's tone whether he or she is bullish, bearish, or on the fence.

Abe Cohen's Brainchild

Investors Intelligence (Larchmont, NY 10558, $72 per year) is the oldest investment "newsletter on newsletters," having been founded in 1963 by the late Abraham W. Cohen. Focusing primarily on the stock market, Investors Intelligence monitors 123 investment services. Each week, the newsletter's editors report the percentage of advisers who are bullish, bearish, or looking for a correction (a temporary interruption in the market's primary trend).

The twenty-year history of the Investors Intelligence poll confirms what a contrarian would expect. The largest percentage of advisers are bullish (optimistic) on the stock market at the top, when prices are about to come down. The bearish (pessimistic) contingent is largest at the bottom, when prices are about to turn up. In short, most advisers—like their followers—lean the wrong way at important market turning points.

Historically, a reading above 60 percent on the bearish scale has nearly always marked the bottom of a primary bear market. As you can see from Figure 2, the Dow Jones industrial average made a triple bottom at the end of the 1981–82 bear market—once in March 1982, again in June, and again in August. The bearish sentiment was strongest at the March low (61 percent), slightly less intense at the June low (58 percent), and least intense (54 percent) at the final August low. Any of these low points would have presented a good opportunity to buy stocks.

By contrast, only 11 percent of the advisers were bearish in June 1983, when most stocks were making their highs for the bull market. Bulls outnumbered bears by almost a 5 to 1 margin. Just when most advisers were convinced that the market could only go up, stock prices stalled, and many high tech and other speculative stocks were beaten down 60, 70, or 80 percent.

The scholarly editors of the Bank Credit Analyst (3463 Peel St., Montreal, Que. H3A 1W7, $445 per year) have devised a helpful way to look at the Investors Intelligence figures. The Bank Credit Analyst takes the percentage of bulls and divides it by the sum of bulls and

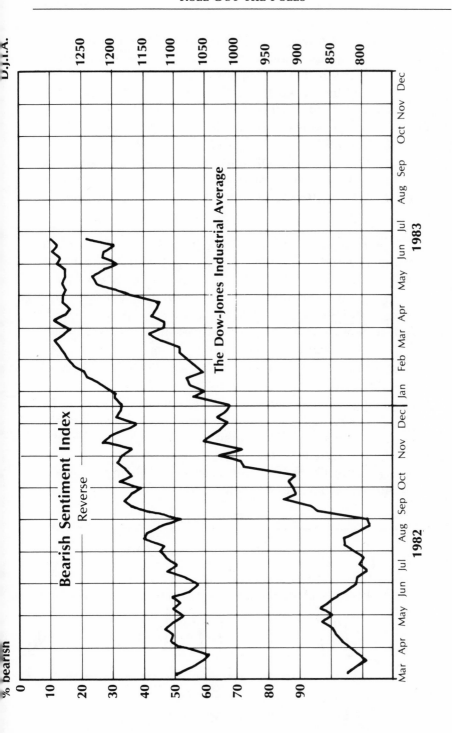

*Vertical lines represent five-week intervals.

Source: Investors Intelligence, Larchmont, N.Y. 10538

Fig. 2.   Bearish sentiment index

bears. Essentially, this maneuver gives you "bulls as a percentage of those willing to express a firm opinion." It ignores the middle-of-the-roaders who are calling for a correction.

To smooth out the weekly fluctuations in the data, the *Bank Credit Analyst* plots a ten-week moving average. (A ten-week moving average is simply an average of the most recent ten weeks' readings; each week, you drop the eleventh week back and add the newest weekly reading.) Figure 3, which depicts this ten-week average of advisory sentiment, shows how far off base the majority usually is at important market turning points. Here are several conclusions you can draw from the chart:

- *A reading above 75 percent is likely to accompany a primary top* in a powerful bull market. This was the case in early 1973 and at three points in 1976. Long-term investors would have been smart to dispose of all their stocks at these junctures. Such lofty readings can also signal an intermediate peak in a strong bull market, as in 1971. Over the past fifteen years, whenever bullish sentiment has climbed above 70 percent, investors who sold their stocks immediately have been able to buy them back at significantly cheaper prices in less than a year.

- *A reading below 35 percent is likely to indicate a primary bottom,* as in 1974, 1978, and 1982. Stocks were a screaming buy at these points. In late 1979, the spring of 1980, and the fall of 1981, these extremely low readings marked an intermediate bottom with excellent opportunities for the nimble investor to earn profits over a three- to six-month period.

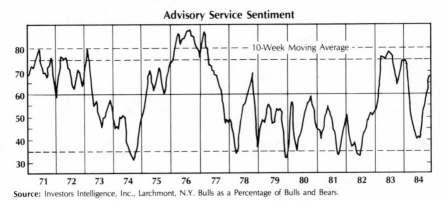

Advisory Service Sentiment

Source: Investors Intelligence, Inc., Larchmont, N.Y. Bulls as a Percentage of Bulls and Bears.

Fig. 3.   Advisory service sentiment

- *A drop from 75 percent to 60 percent early in a bull market represents a normal correction.* In a dynamic primary bull market, it isn't necessary for the bullish percentage to shrink drastically before the market can go on to new highs. In 1971 and 1975, for example, serious pullbacks occurred within powerful primary bull markets. Both times, the bullish consensus tumbled from over 75 percent to about 60 percent on a ten-week basis. A sizable group of nervous advisers threw in the towel and concluded that a major downturn had begun. At that point, the market resumed its advance and promptly climbed to new high ground.

The 1983–84 correction was more severe than the 1971 and 1975 versions, dragging the bullish consensus down to 40 percent by June 1984. To a contrarian, this dramatic shrinkage in the bullish contingent suggested the possibility of a good rally— which arrived in late July 1984. But the bullish reading shot up quickly to 70 percent in November, putting a lid on the market's gains. Apparently, a lot of advisers who failed to anticipate the market's big 1982–83 surge didn't want to be left behind a second time.

Statistical tools like the *Investors Intelligence* poll provide you with an objective yardstick for measuring the market's mood. But no index or formula can eliminate human judgment. You must still exercise discretion when you *interpret* the figures, as you will see if you take another glance at Figure 3. From early 1979 to early 1983—a four-year period—the percentage of bulls never rose above 60. If you had hung on to your stocks in the belief that the bullish consensus would rise to 75 percent or more before the market peaked, you would have been obliged to sit through the mini-crashes of late 1979 and early 1980, as well as the destructive primary bear market of 1981–82.

Rapid inflation and high interest rates in the late 1970s and early 1980s subdued Wall Street's natural optimism. As a result, the bullish ranks never expanded to their traditional limit. The contrary investor must always watch for longer-lasting shifts in the climate of opinion that might push the upper limit for the sentiment index either higher or lower.

A nagging problem with opinion polls of all types is that different pollsters come up with different results. However, if the same person conducts a poll over many years, you should at least be able to compare the results at different points in time. Abe Cohen, founder of *Investors Intelligence*, died in 1983. But his longtime assistant, Michael Burke, has taken over the reins—an assurance that the new figures will continue to be comparable with the old. For the contrarian who plans to commit serious money to the stock market, *Investors Intelligence* is an indispensable timing aid.

Commodity Weather Vane

Like *Investors Intelligence* in the stock market, Earl Hadady's weekly *Market Vane* newsletter (61 S. Lake Ave., Pasadena, CA 91101, $345 per year) tracks the opinions of commodity advisers. *Market Vane* scans approximately 100 sources of professional commodity-trading recommendations, including about thirty market letters published by the leading commission houses (Merrill Lynch, Drexel Burnham, Clayton Brokerage, and so on).

Hadady, who has been running *Market Vane* since 1974, has made several notable refinements in the polling techniques pioneered by *Investors Intelligence*. For one thing, *Market Vane* weights each adviser according to his or her estimated audience. "Obviously, more traders follow the recommendations of the analysts of large brokerage firms than those of smaller firms," Hadady explains.[1] For independent market analysts who publish their own advisory letters, Hadady uses the size of each analyst's subscriber list to estimate how many traders the adviser influences.

By weighting the advisers in proportion to their influence, Hadady ensures that an opinion held by a large number of relatively small (uninfluential) advisory services will not distort his figures. He also grades each adviser on a nine-point scale from 0 (extremely bearish) to 8 (extremely bullish). No other poll in either stock or commodity markets attempts to measure advisory sentiment so precisely.

Market Vane calculates this weighted index or "bullish consensus" on a scale of 0 to 100 percent. A reading of 0 means that everyone is unequivocally bearish and expecting prices to move lower. Fifty percent is neutral, while 100 percent means that everyone is unreservedly bullish and expecting prices to move higher.

Most of the time, the bullish consensus fluctuates between 30 and 70 percent. "At 30 percent," Hadady notes, "an oversold condition is beginning to develop, whereas at 70 percent an overbought condition is developing."[2] In this context, *oversold* means that there are too many underfinanced bears in the marketplace, hoping to make a killing if prices drop. *Overbought* means that there are too many thinly margined bulls who are hoping to make a fortune if prices rise. (Hadady argues that the well-financed "big money" always wins, on balance, in the commodity pits.)

As the consensus approaches the extremes of 0 or 100 percent, an imminent price reversal becomes more and more likely. Once prices have turned around, the bullish consensus will follow suit. The percentage of bulls will rise as the market bounces back from an oversold extreme, and will fall as the market retreats from an overbought extreme.

Waves of Sentiment

No market goes straight up or down. Prices rise or fall in waves. In a primary bull market, the waves tend to form a pattern of higher peaks (and higher troughs, or low points). Likewise, in a primary bear market, the waves tend to peak at successively lower levels while the troughs tend to bottom at successively lower levels. In fact, you can also observe a pattern of ascending or descending waves when the market undergoes a significant intermediate correction against the primary trend, lasting from a few months to a year.

Figure 4 illustrates this wave phenomenon. The primary bull market for gold that began in 1976 reached a climactic peak at $850 in January 1980. From that point onward, gold entered a declining phase that carried the price down to $297 in June 1982. During this twenty-nine-month primary bear market, the price of gold formed a series of lower peaks and lower troughs.

After gold made a primary bear market low in June 1982, the price climbed steeply to $510 in February 1983. During this period, gold traced out a series of higher peaks and troughs. As I write, most analysts are convinced that this upswing was not the beginning of a new primary bull market for gold because, as you can see, the price clearly broke through its upward trendline in February 1983 and headed lower for the next two years.

My own interpretation is that gold merely suffered a severe reaction in 1983–84 against a primary bull trend that is likely to resume and carry the price much higher in 1985–86. The sharp run-up in late 1982 and early 1983 made such a relapse almost inevitable. But regardless

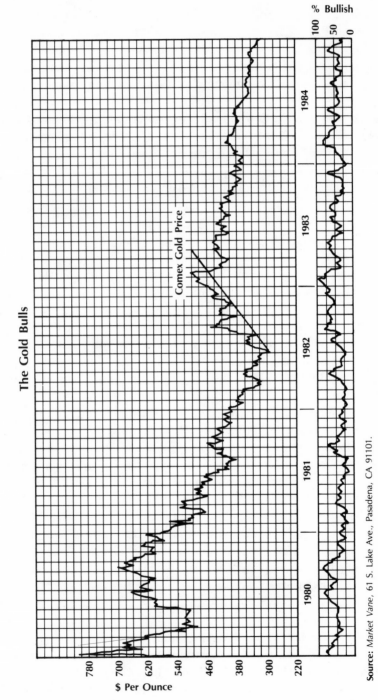

Fig. 4.   The gold bulls

Source: *Market Vane,* 61 S. Lake Ave., Pasadena, CA 91101.

of how you interpret gold's behavior recently—an intermediate correction in a bull market, or the continuation of a primary bear market—the wave pattern is clear.

Advisory sentiment follows the same wavelike pattern as the market. Since most investment advisers are trend followers, their outlook typically grows more cheerful as prices rise and more gloomy as prices fall. Figure 4, which is based on data from *Market Vane*, shows how the percentage of advisers who were bullish on gold gradually declined between 1980 and 1982 as the primary bear market wore on.

After gold prices started to rally from the primary bottom, the bullish consensus rose—in a series of waves—from 17 percent in June 1982 to 88 percent in January 1983. At that point, both the bullish consensus and the price of gold declined in waves until the bottom of the intermediate correction was apparently reached in December 1984.

The correlation between prices and advisory sentiment isn't perfect. (For example, the percentage of gold bulls was higher in June 1982 than in March 1982, even though the price of gold had sunk to a lower low.) But the link is remarkably close. If you trade commodities, you can greatly improve your odds of success by adopting a contrarian strategy based on the *Market Vane* index.

Contrarian Trading Rules

The same basic rules apply to any commodity from gold and silver to pork bellies and Treasury bonds.

- *If the bullish consensus goes above 80 percent or below 20 percent, you should immediately position yourself against the prevailing trend.* A sharp price reversal is imminent. For example, if the consensus on Treasury bonds climbs to 84 percent (as it did in May 1983, when the bond market was forming a major peak), you should sell the bonds short. If the consensus drops to 20 (as it did twice when the market became deeply oversold in May–June 1984), you should buy with both hands.

  Readings above 80 or below 20 are rare. When I recently sifted through six years of *Market Vane* data (1977 to 1982), representing over 7500 consensus readings on thirty-one commodities, I discovered that only 5 percent of the weekly figures were above 80 and less than 4 percent fell below 20. In other words, the typical commodity achieves a bullish consensus above 80 percent or below 20 percent only about twice a year.

- *Until the consensus reaches the 80/20 extremes, you should trade with the prevailing trend.* As Humphrey Neill, the "Vermont ruminator," used to say, "The public is right about the trends, but wrong at both ends." For illustration, let's assume that the bullish consensus for hogs was 15 percent last week and 23 percent this week. Under the 80/20 rule, you should have bought a hog contract last week when the consensus reached an oversold extreme. You should now hold the contract until the consensus stops rising.

Of course, the consensus may not get all the way down to 20 percent or all the way up to 80 percent. Sometimes the market bottoms with a 25 or 30 percent consensus and peaks with a 70 or 75 percent consensus. Furthermore, even if the consensus reaches the classic extremes, you may not dare (for the moment) to pit yourself against the overconfident majority. Instead, you may decide that you want to wait for some confirmation that the market has turned around. By the time the market has clearly reversed itself, however, the bullish consensus may have jumped to, say, 30 percent (in a rising market) or dropped to perhaps 70 percent (in a falling market).

In such cases, you can still buy at any reading below 30 or sell at any reading above 70, but you should recognize that the odds aren't running quite so strongly in your favor. If, after you enter your trade, the consensus stalls for a couple of weeks at mid-range (40 to 60 percent), you should pull out and wait for the next genuine overbought or oversold extreme. Never play the commodity market when your chances of making a profitable trade appear to be only about 50–50. Those are losers' odds. If you take a 50–50 bet, the professional floor traders, who have access to information that you don't and can react faster than you, will nearly always edge you out.

- *In a strong primary bull or bear market, a short-term correction won't usually carry the consensus down to 20 percent or up to 80 percent.* Look back at Figure 4. During 1981, a bearish year for gold, the consensus never rose above 71 percent (the September peak). In fact, the March, May, and December peaks for the consensus were all in the 40 to 50 percent range. By the same token, when gold was rising sharply in the second half of 1982, the lowest point that the consensus attained was 35 percent (at the August trough). The October and November lows were around 50 percent.

In general, a short-term reaction in a strong bull or bear market will reverse itself and the primary trend will resume when the consensus moves into the 40 to 60 percent range. In a powerful bull market, you should buy (go along) when the consensus retreats from the overbought area to mid-range. Likewise, in a powerful bear market, you should sell short when the consensus bounces up from an oversold area to mid-range. Figure 5 illustrates this principle.

In most cases, you shouldn't try to trade against the primary trend in a vigorous bull or bear market. The dips in a bull market are usually too brief and too shallow for short selling, just as most rallies in a bear market are too ephemeral and too weak for snatching profits on the long side.

However, every primary bull or bear market eventually comes to an end. In addition, many primary markets undergo severe intermediate reactions or corrections that bring the consensus down to 20 (or below) on the low side or up to 80 (or above) on the high side. You can tell that the primary trend is about to change, or that a severe intermediate reaction is about to set in, when the bullish consensus goes to an 80/20 extreme *and stays there for three to five weeks in a row*. Markets simply cannot sustain an extreme degree of optimism or pessimism for long. A sharp swing in the opposite direction nearly always ensues.

Even if you don't regularly trade commodities, the *Market Vane* index provides valuable information for long-term investors in stocks, bonds, currencies, and precious metals. Futures contracts tied to several major stock indexes (the Standard & Poor's 500, the New York Stock Exchange Composite, and the Value Line Composite) have been trading since 1982, joining the older financial-futures contracts on Treasury bills, notes, and bonds, bank CDs, foreign currencies, and precious metals.

Each of these futures contracts has a bullish consensus you can track for signs of an important buying or selling opportunity. For example, the string of low readings for gold in June 1982 sent out a buy signal for all forms of gold, not merely futures contracts but also phys-

Bullish Consensus Meter

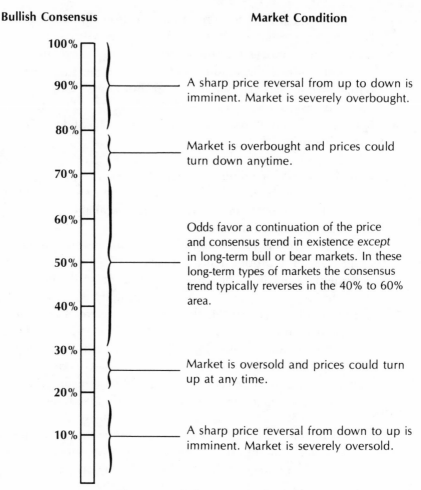

Fig. 5. Bullish consensus meter

58

ical bullion and mining shares. Similarly, the sky-high readings for Treasury bonds in April and May 1983 (averaging almost 80 percent over a four-week period) provided a timely sell signal for *all* bonds; Treasuries, corporates, and municipals.

My rule for long-term investors is simple. If the bullish consensus averages more than 75 percent over a four-week period, sell. The market is probably making a peak that won't be seen again for many months, perhaps years. If the consensus averages less than 25 percent over a four-week period, the market is begging you to buy.

Informal Polls

The *Investors Intelligence* and *Market Vane* polls are two of the most reliable guides to what investment professionals and, by extension, their clients are thinking. The *Wall Street Journal* also takes a somewhat informal, but nonetheless revealing, poll of commodity advisers every six months. Lately, the *Journal* has been publishing its semiannual surveys in January and July.

While the *Journal* poll is conducted too infrequently to be of value as a short-term timing device, it can give you a clue to *which markets you should avoid* over the intermediate term (the next six months). A commodity that appears at the top of the *Journal's* buy list is almost guaranteed to go down.

In January 1983, for instance, the *Journal* headline proclaimed: "Copper and Gold Futures Top Choices of Experts." Copper drew 18 votes from the panel of experts, followed by 16 for gold, and 15 for foreign currencies.[3] Five weeks later, both copper and gold (along with most other metals) nose-dived. Foreign currencies began to collapse almost as soon as the ink was dry on the article. Everyone who had followed the advice of the *Journal's* poll of investment sages would have lost their shirts.

The favorites of the July 1983 survey performed scarcely better. Soybeans led the list with 15 votes, trailed by stock indexes with 13, and sugar with 11 votes.[4] All three commodities had climbed sharply in the weeks just before the survey, convincing trend followers that something big was afoot.

The result? Six months later, soybeans had gone nowhere, while you would have lost $5500 per contract on the Value Line Stock Index, and $4000 per contract on sugar.

More recently, in January 1984, the *Journal* told us: "Paper Investments Are Top Choice of Futures Panel for '84 First Half." Foreign currencies came in first with 20 votes, while stock indexes and Treasury bonds tied for second place with 15 votes.[5] By midyear, the stock indexes and Treasury bonds had crashed, confirming that the *Journal* poll has indeed earned a niche in the pantheon of contrary indicators. (If you had followed the *Journal* panel's advice on Treasury bonds, you would have lost a whopping $10,000 per contract.) Foreign currencies, after a brief rally in February and March, fell back to their January levels and netted nothing for speculators who took their cue from the *Journal* poll.

You can devise your own informal poll of investment advisers if you subscribe to a representative sampling of financial newsletters. While many newsletter writers acknowledge the power of contrary thinking (at least in theory), few attempt to practice it consistently. Most simply follow the prevailing market trend. If the market is going up, they tell their subscribers to buy; if the market is going down, they recommend selling.

This strategy has at least one virtue. Because the adviser changes his tune with every twist and turn of the market, he never appears to be drastically wrong. (As the old saying goes: If you can't predict, predict often.) To be sure, he seldom helps his subscribers make any big profits. But he reinforces their emotional penchant to buy after prices have risen, and to sell after the market has fallen—to buy high and sell low. Since he is a kindred spirit and massages their psyches, they renew their subscriptions.

Fortunately, you can conduct your own private, thoroughly unscientific poll without wading through seventy or eighty investment newsletters. Select four or five publications, preferably written by advisers with a fondness for brash or flamboyant statements, or by "pure" technicians who believe that trendlines and chart patterns tell all. These advisers (who shall remain nameless to protect the guilty!) are most likely to get swept up in the emotions of the crowd when a powerful market trend is approaching a climactic reversal. Here are some of the signals letter writers will send you at important market turning points:

- *Longtime bulls will suddenly turn bearish* at the bottom. Bears will predict a further price collapse of 30 to 40 percent. The few bulls who don't turn bearish will sharply lower their forecasts.
- *Diehard bears will turn bullish* at the top, while bulls will make

outrageously optimistic projections. The few timid bears who remain won't dare to advise short selling (when the risk is nil).

- *Normally cautious bears will recommend short selling* and other aggressive tactics at the bottom. At the top, normally cautious bulls will urge you to speculate (with low-priced stocks, futures contracts, options, margin accounts, etc.).

- *Technicians will cite heavy trading volume* at the top as evidence that the market is headed higher. "Over 160 million shares can't be wrong!" was a typical adviser's misguided comment on the stock market in early January 1984, just before the Dow industrials collapsed 165 points. The same technicians will pooh-pooh low trading volume at the bottom because they will be looking for a "selling climax."

- *Chartists will worry about broken trendlines*, violated moving averages, and "downside confirmation" at the bottom. The same analysts will blithely reassure you at the top that all is well because the Dow, or pork bellies, or gold (you name it), is trading above its trendlines and moving averages, and indeed has just climbed to a new high.

Whether you make your own informal survey of advisory opinion or subscribe to one of the polling services, the stark fact remains that *most investment advisers are wrong precisely when it pays the most to be right*—at primary and important intermediate turning points for the market. How can "professionals" with such awful records stay in business? As an investment adviser myself, I am tempted to plead the Fifth.

But the answer to this paradox, it seems to me, is that the better advisers don't stay wrong for long. They are flexible enough to recognize a mistake and to reverse themselves before their clients suffer irrecoverable losses. As a result, *most* of the time, *most* advisers are *more or less* right about the market—at least about the primary trend. If you want to rise above this mediocrity, you must buy and sell when market sentiment reaches its greatest extremes: when most advisers are too afraid (at the bottom) or too greedy (at the top) to join you.

5
Stock Market Timing

Ripeness is all.
—Shakespeare

In selecting the soundest financial investments, the question of when to buy is far more important than what to buy.
—Roger W. Babson

Happiness is a stock that goes up when the rest of the market is going down. Nothing makes you feel more intelligent, more self-satisfied, more disdainful of the millions who are wringing their hands while the Dow Jones averages plummet day after day.

On the other hand, nothing is quite so infuriating as a stock that refuses to budge when the rest of the board is racing ahead. It makes you feel like a fool, an incompetent—an amateur. "You could have picked better stocks by throwing darts at the newspaper," you ruefully remind yourself.

Anybody who plays the market for long will occasionally experience delight, or disappointment, when a stock travels in the opposite direction from the market. Just as Republicans on Capitol Hill sometimes vote for Democrat-sponsored measures (and vice versa), every stock is to some extent a free agent, marching to its own drumbeat.

Gold shares, for example, rose during the 1929–32 market crash, while the Dow Jones industrial average plunged 89 percent. Or, to take a recent contrasting case: At the Dow's November 1983 high, after the average had mounted a breathtaking 60-percent rise in fifteen months, two dozen stocks listed on the Big Board reached new lows for the year.

My intent, however, isn't to show how perverse the stock market can be. Quite the contrary. These are the exceptions that prove the rule: *Most of the time, most stocks go up or down together.* Of course, not every stock, every day, follows the same path as the major market averages (the Dow industrials, the Standard & Poor's 500, the Value Line Composite, etc.). In fact, it isn't unusual, even on a day when the major averages move strongly in one direction, to find that a quarter to a third of all issues with price changes darted off in the opposite direction.

But if the market averages follow a sustained trend for many weeks or months, the great majority of stocks will do likewise. Looking for stocks that will go up in a bear market is as thankless a task as looking for stocks that will go down in a bull market. Unless you consider yourself a genius, I don't suggest that you attempt it.

During the 1980–82 primary downswing, for instance, about 80 percent of the industrial shares on the New York Stock Exchange (NYSE) were worth less at the August 1982 lows than at the November 1980 highs. Thus, your chances of selecting a winner that would have bucked this downtrend were approximately one in five, and the 1980–82 bear market was remarkably less severe than most. In the famous smash of 1973–74, over 95 percent of the stocks on the NYSE declined.

Market Timing or Stock Selection?

Some Wall Street sages maintain that it is impossible to detect major bull or bear markets in advance. Therefore, the argument runs, you should always remain fully invested in stocks that appear to be good long-term values. "Don't try to time the market," these people advise. "Just select the right stocks and you'll come out ahead in the long run."

Most brokers, securities analysts, *Forbes* columnists, and others who tout stocks for a living display a fondness for this point of view. It isn't difficult to see why. What would your broker do to stay busy during the long months of a primary bear market if he or she didn't think that *some* stock *somewhere* is always a good buy? Your broker could urge you to profit from falling prices by selling short, I suppose, but most of them regard short selling as too risky.*

*In a short sale, you borrow stock from your broker and sell it. Naturally, you must eventually return the borrowed stock. But if the market price of the stock drops after the short sale, you can buy the stock back (*cover the short*)

64

Market timing is probably an inappropriate strategy for big institutions, which require weeks, even months, to build up or liquidate their massive stock portfolios. (If an institution buys too much stock too quickly, it pushes prices up; if it sells too much too quickly, it pushes prices down.) Some institutions with a contrarian philosophy have compiled successful, long-term track records by selecting low-risk, out-of-favor stocks without regard for broad market movements.

A fine example of this species is United Bank of Denver (1700 Broadway, Denver, CO 80217, 303-861-8811). United Bank's commingled trust fund for corporate pension and profit-sharing plans rolled up a compound annual gain of 26 percent in the five years ended December 31, 1983—a dazzling record for a bank trust department, comparable to the performance of the best "quality" growth mutual funds.

This superior showing resulted from United's strategy of buying *deeply undervalued* stocks (with low price-to-earnings ratios and price-to-book-value ratios). The bank remains fully invested just about all the time, and holds for the long term (typically three years). A similar fund for personal trust customers has performed almost as well as the pension fund; it is open to individuals with $20,000 or more to invest.

In Chapter 6, I will discuss in detail several contrarian strategies for choosing your own stocks. Contrary thinking, however, can also give you an edge when you are trying to spot important turning points for the market as a whole. If you can correctly identify the market's primary trend, almost any diversified portfolio of fifteen to twenty-five stocks will ring up profits for you, even if you make your selections by lobbing darts at the stock tables in your newspaper!

As a matter of fact, if you learn the art of market timing, you can dispense with selecting individual stocks. A mutual fund, which represents a diversified portfolio, will do the job for you. All you need to know is when to buy shares of the fund, and when to sell them.

In previous chapters, I explained how to spot important reversals in the stock market by analyzing the comments of market gurus quoted in your daily newspaper. I also described the *Investors Intelligence* poll and how to interpret it. Now let's focus on some of the less-well-known,

for less than the price you received when you sold it short. A short seller profits from a *decline* in the price of a stock. However, since the stock could theoretically rise to infinity, saddling you with an infinite loss, many brokers steer away from short selling.

and often more precise, contrary indicators that can point you to major buying and selling opportunities.

Year in and year out, certain groups of investors consistently do well while others, with equal regularity, fare poorly. For convenience, I call these groups the *smart money* and the *dumb money*. The smart money buys low and sells high, while the dumb money does just the opposite.

Smart-money investors tend to be successful Wall Street professionals who trade stock for a living, or well-heeled amateurs who buy stocks and hold them for the long term. These people typically have a good sense of value—the mark of a true contrarian. The dumb money, on the other hand, generally consists of amateur short-term speculators—in-and-out traders—who are looking for a quick profit. They go where the action is, and usually hop on the trolley right at the end of the line.

If you want to join the winner's circle in the stock market, I suggest that you follow a simple axiom: Do what the smart money is doing, and do exactly the opposite of what the dumb money is doing. When the smart money is buying, you buy; but when the dumb money is buying, you sell. Likewise, when the smart money is selling, you sell; but when the dumb money is selling, you buy. At significant turning points, these two groups are nearly always poles apart in their thinking.

But who is the smart money and who is the dumb money?

America's Most Knowledgeable Investors

When it comes to recognizing the primary trend, the shrewdest group of stock market investors in America is probably the *corporate insiders*—officers and directors of publicly traded companies. Nobody has ever investigated whether these corporate bigwigs are more adept than other investors at managing their entire portfolios. But the insiders certainly do much better than the public at trading *shares of their own companies*—partly because the insiders know more about their companies than the best-informed securities analysts, and partly because federal law requires insiders to take a long-term view of the markets.

Insiders aren't allowed to sell their company's stock until six months have elapsed since their last purchase (and vice versa if they wish to buy). In addition, if insiders acquire their stock at bargain prices through a company stock-option plan, they are required to hang on to the stock for at least two years. These provisions of the law discourage short-term trading and encourage insiders to focus on long-term values.

Federal securities law also prohibits insiders from buying or selling their company's stock on the basis of *material* information not known to the public. (Supposedly, any piece of news that might significantly affect the price of the stock is material.) Hence, if you were the president of XYZ company, it would be illegal to buy XYZ stock if you knew that another firm was about to make a takeover offer for XYZ. In the same vein, it would be illegal to sell your shares if you knew that XYZ was about to announce a huge loss.

However, a lot of *nonmaterial* but valuable information passes through the hands of insiders day after day, week after week. The chairman or president of a corporation, who usually sees his firm's daily or weekly sales reports and knows when the company is working on a new product or negotiating a big contract, can form an accurate picture of the company's earnings prospects long before an official announcement is made.

Furthermore, members of the board of directors, even though they may not work full time for the corporation, can pick up helpful tidbits from conversations with management. Studies have shown that all insiders, the chairman, president, and directors typically make the most profitable judgments about buying or selling a company's stock.[1]

As a rule of thumb, stocks heavily purchased by insiders outperform the market averages by about 2 to 1 in a bull market, and fall half as fast in a bear market. Stocks with heavy insider selling, on the other hand, tend to rise only half as much as the market averages when the primary trend is up, and fall twice as hard when the primary trend is down. In Chapter 6, I discuss insider trading as a tool for selecting individual stocks to buy or sell.

However, insider trading is also a revealing indicator of the market's general direction. When the market averages are close to an important bottom, insiders as a group swing to the buy side; when the averages are approaching a significant top, the insiders sell heavily. Figure 6 documents this remarkable correlation.

Over the past ten years, whenever insider purchases, as a percentage of total insider trades, exceeded 50 percent (i.e., there were more purchases than sales), the market was forming a good bottom. At the 1974 lows, which presented the best buying opportunity in twenty-five years, insider purchases soared to 73 percent of all trades.

By contrast, insider sales outnumbered purchases by a 4 to 1 margin—

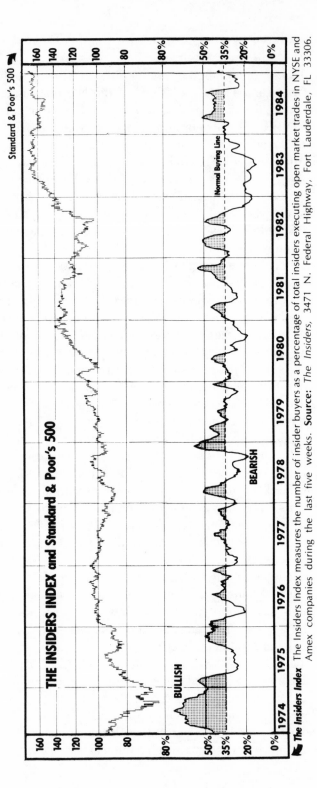

Fig. 6. Insider sell/buy ratio

the insiders index dipped to 20 percent—at the important market peaks in 1976, 1978, and 1980. During the orgy of speculation that marked the June 1983 top, insider selling reached epidemic proportions. One week, sales outweighed purchases by a 9 to 1 count. Small wonder that the most overheated sectors of the market—the high tech stocks and the glamorous over-the-counter growth stocks generally—nose-dived soon afterward.

You will note, if you study the chart, that the insiders actually began unloading heavily in the last few months of 1982. Some analysts cite this fact as evidence that the insiders were premature in their selling. But were they, really? By the time the long 1983–84 setback was over, hundreds of stocks on all exchanges were trading well below their prices in November 1982, when the insiders began to bail out. No, the insiders were right on target: They sensed from the outset that the market's sharp advance in the first half of 1983 (from roughly 1000 to 1250 on the Dow) was built on sand.

An interesting feature of the last few months on the chart is the sharp swing from heavy insider selling in June 1983 to fairly intense buying in mid–1984—the strongest buying, in fact, since the major market lows of the spring and summer of 1982. Sure enough, the market exploded in late July and early August 1984. But then "America's most knowledgeable investors" (as editor Norman Fosback of *The Insiders* calls them) swung back to the sell side. The market groaned, wheezed, and stalled.

Several newsletters are specifically devoted to monitoring and interpreting insider activity in the stock market. They include:

- *The Insiders* (3471 N. Federal Hwy., Ft. Lauderdale, FL 33306; fortnightly, $100 a year). Ranks stocks according to "insider ratings" and keeps tabs on marketwide insider trading for timing purposes.

- *Insiders Chronicle* (P.O. Box 272977, Boca Raton, FL 33427; weekly, $325 a year). Lists all significant insider trades on NYSE, AMEX, and OTC. In-depth articles analyzing companies with heavy insider buying.

- *Consensus of Insiders* (P.O. Box 24349, Ft. Lauderdale, FL 33307; weekly, $247 a year). Editor Perry Wysong's portfolio of insider stocks has gained over 1000 percent since 1962, versus 79 percent for the Dow industrials.

69

- *Insider Indicator* (2230 N.E. Brazee St., Portland, OR 97212; bi-weekly, $145 per year). Edited by Mike Reid, this newsletter ranked among the top 5 percent in the nation, according to a recent survey by Select Information Exchange, an organization that rates the performance of investment advisers. Has a particularly fine record for selecting individual stocks.

The Members' Club

Besides the corporate insiders, some Wall Street professionals belong to the elite fraternity of smart money. Member firms of the stock exchanges make good profits, on balance, when trading for their own account—although too often they seem to lose the knack when trading for your account!

To read the minds of the members, you can turn each week to the "Market Laboratory" section of *Barron's*, a daunting page of statistics that probably carries a greater quantity of useful information than the rest of the newspaper combined. Figure 7 shows a portion of the "Market Laboratory" page with the data you need.

Under the heading "NYSE volume report," you will notice that *Barron's* prints the total number of shares sold short during the most recent reporting week, together with the number of shares sold short by the member firms. (The New York Stock Exchange releases the numbers with a two-week delay, but the information is usually current enough to give you an accurate picture of what these professionals are thinking.) Divide the member shorts by the total shorts, and express the result as a percent. This figure is known as the *member-short ratio*.

The members are usually right about the direction the market is going to take over the intermediate to long term. When these savvy operators are selling short at a breakneck pace (betting that prices will fall), you would be well advised to sell with them. Contrariwise, when the members cut back on their short selling, you can infer that they are expecting stock quotes to rise. Step up to the counter and buy!

A reading above 87 percent on the member-short ratio (see Figure 8) is a screaming sell signal for the intermediate term and often signals a reversal of the primary trend as well. In late May 1983, the most recent upper extreme, the member-short ratio leaped to 89 percent, warning that the market was grossly overbought. The vast majority of NYSE

BARRON'S MARKET LABORATORY

Week's Market Statistics

	Last week	Prev. week	Last year
Sales NYSE, th sh	472,389	416,430	347,226
Sales AMEX, th sh	31,800	31,810	30,540
Sales OTC, th sh-a	326,044	287,421	290,845
Sales Dow Indus, th sh	58,573	44,929	39,054
Sales Dow Transp, th sh	13,590	13,777	13,522
Sales Dow Utils, th sh	12,105	7,320	6,189
Sales Dow Comp, th sh	84,268	66,026	58,765
Bond offerings, th $-v	3,905,601	3,912,330	2,590,300
Stock offerings, th $-v	335,653	523,842	719,770
Low Price Stk. Index-v	238.87	237.94	263.06
Volume, th sh	1,419.0	2,214.2	1,557.0
%vol to DJI vol	2.37	3.83	4.06
20 Most Active Stocks:			
Average price	40.21	37.68	42.08
% vol to total vol	16.32	17.28	14.93

NYSE volume report, Aug. 10:			
Buy/sell, th sh-w	756,253	698,547	380,781
Total shorts, th sh	96,487.6	81,333.0	30,256.7
Public shorts, th sh	15,687.7	14,906.3	4,833.3
Member trading, Aug. 10:			
Member shrt, th sh-x	80,799.8	66,426.7	25,423.4
Speclst shrt, th sh	44,529.7	34,374.5	12,869.3
Purchases, th sh	230,728.5	174,759.4	112,546.0
Sales,th sh-z	244.161.8	205,019.6	112,983.1
Net buy/sell, th sh	-13,433.3	-30,260.2	-437.1
% vol to NYSE vol	31.40	27.18	29.61
Odd-lot trading, Aug. 10:			

	Last week	Prev. week	Last year
Purchases, th sh	1,708	1,550	1,478
Purchases, th $	60,466	50,173	60,671
Sales, th sh-z	5,375	4,022	2,707
Sales, th $	216,561	154,582	107,506
Short sales, actual	8,228	12,654	8,105
Bond vol, NYSE, th $	116,944	120,680	109,640
Best Grade Bonds %-y	12.40	12.43	11.32
Intrm Grade Bonds %-y	13.64	13.73	12.64
Confidence Index-c	90.9	90.5	89.6
Stock/Bond Yield Gap-s	-7.73	-7.67	-6.66
Yield Returns on Dow-Jones Averages:			
30 Industrials, %	4.67	4.76	4.66
20 Transports, %.	2.65	2.68	2.72
15 Utilities, %	10.35	10.43	9.72
20 Bonds, %-y	13.40	13.47	12.16
10 Utils, %-y	13.95	14.15	12.82
10 Indus, %-y	12.85	12.79	11.50
Bond Buyers' 20 Muni			
Bond Index, %-y	10.02	10.02	9.59

a-NASDAQ. c-Ratio best grade to intermediate grade bonds. r-Revised. s-Spread between dividend yield on DJI and yield to maturity on best grade bonds. v-Week ended Thursday. w-Shares and warrants. x-Includes specialists short sales. y-Yield to maturity week ended Thursday. z-Includes short sales.

Fig. 7.   Barron's market laboratory

stocks made their highs for the year a few weeks later and a few Dow points higher.

Normally, a reading below 78 percent on the member-short ratio signals an upturn in the market's intermediate trend. A dramatic drop in member-short selling can also coincide with the beginning of a primary bull market, as in August 1982 (see Figure 8). But the member-short ratio gave a false buy signal in December 1983, when many Wall Street firms, apparently as a ploy to defer income taxes into 1984, cut back on their year-end short selling.

No indicator is infallible, but, because of this disappointing expe-

The Member Short Sale Ratio

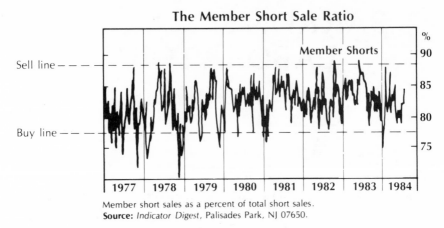

Member short sales as a percent of total short sales.
Source: *Indicator Digest*, Palisades Park, NJ 07650.

Fig. 8.   Member-short ratio

rience, I suggest that you handle the member-short ratio with extra care. If it is sending the same message as the other contrary indicators, treat it with respect. If, on the other hand, it is out of sync with the rest of the evidence, don't be too alarmed. This indicator has strayed off the reservation before.

Wall Street's Wrong-Way Corrigans

When the insiders take a strong stand on the stock market, bullish or bearish, time usually proves them right. Ditto with the stock exchange's members. Unfortunately, though, many other groups of investors aren't nearly so successful. In fact, I can state categorically: *When the public engages in fast-buck speculation (short selling and options trading are the best examples), it nearly always loses money in the end.*

The hapless odd-lot short seller is a case in point. This unlucky lad sells irregular units of stock short, typically fewer than 100 shares. He is the classic small-potatoes speculator, completely out of his element in the exciting but dangerous world of short selling. Almost without exception, he steps up his activity at the bottom of the market and ignores the profitable opportunities to sell short at the top.

Figure 9 tells the pitiful story. This graph plots odd-lot short sales as a percent of average odd-lot volume (total odd-lot purchases and sales, divided by two). Since the daily figures can jump around erratically, the graph smooths them out with a five-day moving average.

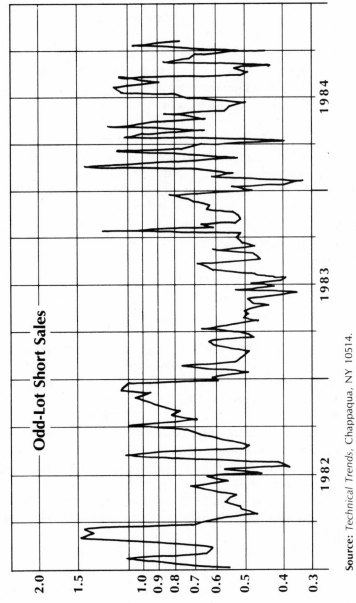

Source: *Technical Trends*, Chappaqua, NY 10514.

Fig. 9. Odd-lot short sales

As you can see, extremely high readings on this indicator (1 percent or more) were recorded at the primary market low of August 1982 and at several intermediate lows before and since. Odd-lot short sales were another sentiment gauge that gave a strongly favorable signal in July 1984, suggesting that a powerful rally was just around the corner.

On the other hand, when the odd-lot short sale indicator reads less than 0.3 percent—as it did at the intermediate market peak in June 1983 and just before the January 1984 massacre—you had better turn defensive. The "odd lotters" are too optimistic, a bad omen indeed for the contrary investor.

The NYSE releases statistics on odd-lot short selling every day, with only a one-day delay, as opposed to the two-week delay with the member shorts. If the market is moving rapidly, investor sentiment will also tend to shift rapidly. For a more up-to-date look at what the public is thinking, keep an eye on the odd-lot statistics, which are published daily in the *New York Times*, *The Wall Street Journal*, and weekly in *Barron's* "Market Laboratory."

Options: A Loser's Game?

Options traders provide what is probably the most dependable market-timing indicator in the whole contrarian galaxy. By nature, people who play the options market tend to be gamblers, dreamers who hope to parlay a couple of thousand dollars into a fortune. As a group (there are many individual exceptions), they represent the dumb money at its dumbest.

There are two types of options. A *call* gives the buyer the right to purchase (call away) 100 shares of a specified stock at a fixed price (the strike price) during the life of the option (never more than nine months). A *put* gives the buyer the right to sell (put) 100 shares of a given stock at the strike price up to the expiration date. Speculators buy calls when they expect a stock to go up; they buy puts when they expect a stock to go down.

Although it is possible to devise a conservative strategy for trading these highly volatile instruments (see Chapter 9), most options speculators take a "go-for-broke" approach, and end up broke as a result. Nonetheless, the rest of us can learn from these losers' mistakes. Their biggest error, which makes them such an interesting study from a contrarian point of view, is that they become increasingly bullish as prices rise, and increasingly bearish as prices fall. Call buying increases when the market is tracing out an important top, while put buying surges when the market is forming a major bottom.

Figure 10 gives you an idea of how the options traders have behaved over the past couple of years. At the primary market bottom in August 1982, speculators were betting their bottom dollar that prices would drop further. The number of calls purchased exceeded puts purchased by a meager 1.18 margin. In perfect contrary style, the market exploded upward. Four similar readings occurred in April, May, June, and July 1984 just before the Dow industrials skyrocketed 160 points.

At the other extreme, euphoric speculators were buying three calls for every put in June 1983. Result: most stocks backpedaled for the next thirteen months, and hundreds of issues collapsed.

To calculate the ratio for yourself, you can refer to the options pages of the *Wall Street Journal*. Although options are traded on several exchanges, the most important market, and the only one you really need to track, is the Chicago Board of Trade. Just divide the call volume for the day by the put volume. Since daily readings can swing up or down quite sharply, I suggest that you keep a ten-day moving average to block out the statistical "noise." (The graph in Figure 10 plots a ten-day average.)

Or, if it is too much trouble for you to consult the *Journal* every day, you can find a summary of the past week's options trading in *Barron's*. By adding together the figures from two issues of *Barron's*, you can quickly compute a ten-day average.

In general, a reading below 1.5 on the ten-day put ratio indicates that an intermediate bottom is at hand, and a reading close to 1.0 suggests a spectacular buying opportunity. But when the ratio climbs above 2.7, you should watch out for a drop in the market. A reading of 3.0 or more, sustained over several weeks, is likely to mean that a sharp downswing lies immediately ahead.

Typically, the call-put ratio, like most sentiment indicators, lingers in overbought territory for stretches of several weeks in the early stages of a bull market; it also wallows deeply in oversold territory for weeks at a time in the late phases of a bear market. Thus, when the trend of the market has been running strongly in one direction for a few months, the cautious investor should wait for several extreme readings, each a few weeks apart, before he or she goes contrary to the options traders. Let them empty their wallets completely before you bet against them!

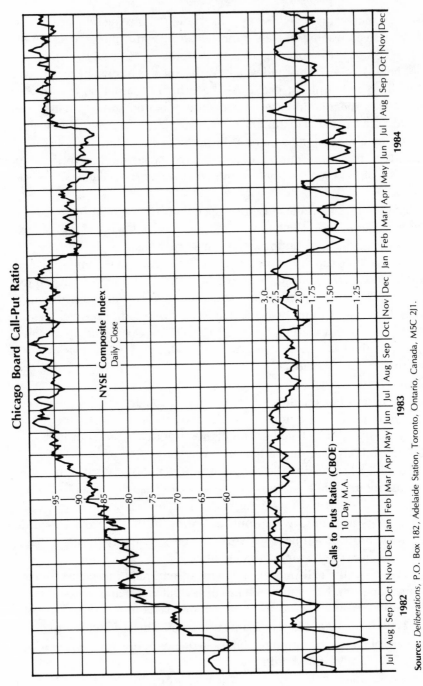

Fig. 10.   CBOE call-put ratio

Source: *Deliberations*, P.O. Box 182, Adelaide Station, Toronto, Ontario, Canada, M5C 2J1.

Our Mutual Friends

Is it fair to include megabuck institutions with the dumb money? As I noted earlier in this chapter, banks, pension funds, mutual funds, and other institutional investors are, for the most part, simply too big to practice market timing successfully over the long term. Nonetheless, many of them try their hand at it. Managers of common-stock mutual funds are notorious for building up their cash holdings just as the market is nearing a significant low. Likewise, mutual funds tend to be fully invested, with minimal cash, near the market's highs.

For a graphic depiction of this phenomenon, take a glance at Figure 11. Since 1966, the mutual funds' cash holdings have regularly peaked at 10 to 12 percent of their assets—right at the bottom of every primary bear market, when calm, rational *contrary* investors should have owned stocks up to their ears!

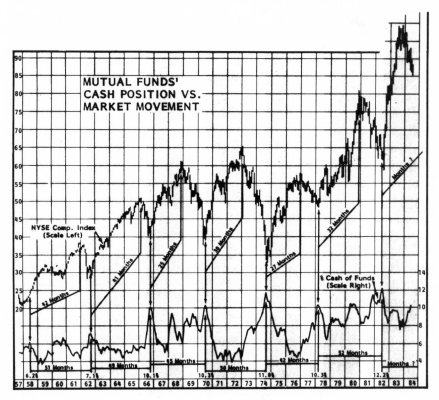

Source: *Growth Fund Guide*, P.O. Box 6600, Rapid City, SD 57709.

Fig. 11.   Mutual funds' cash position

However, this indicator has been somewhat less helpful in calling market tops. Interest rates have risen sharply since the beginning of the Vietnam era, encouraging fund managers to hold more cash throughout the market cycle than they would have felt comfortable with during the "go-go" years of the early 1960s. (With today's high rates, Treasury bills and other risk-free, interest-bearing cash equivalents present formidable competition for common stocks.)

Nonetheless, it seems reasonable to expect that the current bull market will not achieve its final peak until the mutual funds' cash holdings drop to perhaps 6 or 7 percent of assets. In late 1984, the ratio was still running about 9 percent. (*Barron's* publishes the monthly figure on the inside back page under "Economic and Financial Indicators.") Back in the 1960s, and even as recently as 1976, the cash ratio dipped as low as 4 percent at market tops. But back in those days, Treasury bills paid only 3 or 4 percent a year, as opposed to 9 or 10 percent now.

I strongly recommend no-load (no sales charge) mutual funds for investors who want to play the stock market but lack the time, expertise, or money to build and supervise a diversified portfolio. By pooling your stake with that of thousands of other investors, a mutual fund can put together a portfolio of fifty or more stocks—easily a broad enough selection to protect you from a freakish catastrophe in any single company (a plane crash killing the entire executive management, for example).

Many clever strategies have been developed for trading mutual funds. In most cases, these programs rely heavily on technical analysis (trend following). For example, one widely followed system puts you into the market after the Dow Jones industrial average and a composite index of mutual funds rise above their respective thirty-nine-week moving averages. You are supposed to get out when both of these indicators fall below these averages.

The problem with technical programs of this sort, as I have pointed out before, is that they often signal you to buy after prices have already risen substantially and to sell after prices have already fallen substantially. For instance, the system I just described issued a sell signal in late January 1984, after the average aggressive-growth fund had already plunged 20 percent from its June 1983 highs. The system put investors back into the market in August 1984 after the Dow industrials had already risen 120 points from the July lows.

Technical systems also tend to generate a lot of *whipsaws*—rapid in-and-out moves that can frustrate your efforts to earn tax-favored long-term capital gains. (You must hold a stock or mutual fund more than six months to qualify for the lower tax rate on long-term gains.) Unless you plan to trade mutual funds through a tax-sheltered retirement account, I would advise you to avoid these technical programs.

Instead, I recommend a contrarian program for investing in mutual funds that consists of the following simple rules:

Rule 1. *Buy when the market is displaying the signs of a solid primary bottom.* You'll know a primary bottom is at hand when you see the following:

- Panicky newspaper commentary
- High "bearish" readings on the *Investors Intelligence* poll
- Heavy insider buying (including major programs by corporations to buy back their own shares)
- Scanty short selling by members
- Heavy odd-lot short selling
- Low call-put ratio
- Large mutual fund cash reserves

Rule 2. *Sell when the market is showing the characteristics of a primary top:*

- Euphoric newspaper commentary
- High "bullish" readings on the *Investors Intelligence* poll
- Heavy insider selling (including a flood of new issues of stock by corporations)
- Heavy short selling by members
- Negligible odd-lot short selling
- High call-put ratio
- Depleted mutual fund cash reserves

Rule 3. *If you miss the primary bottom or top, wait* for the next intermediate bottom to buy, or the next intermediate top to sell. Most bull markets give you at least two good opportunities to buy, and most bear markets give you at least two good opportunities to sell, typically one to five months after the primary turning point.

For investors who demand an ultra-simple trading system that takes only five minutes a week to monitor and requires no calculations, the Technical Market Index featured on the television show "Wall Street Week" is an extremely sharp contrarian market-timing tool. The index is usually flashed on the screen during the first five minutes of the show. While most viewers seem to watch "Wall Street Week" primarily for the good-natured banter of host Louis Rukeyser and for the stock tips purveyed by his guests, the WSW Index is easily the most valuable information you will find on the program.

Originated by Robert Nurock, editor of *The Astute Investor* (P.O. Box 988, Paoli, PA 19301, $197 per year), the WSW Index actually consists of ten separate indicators rolled into one. Insider activity is one of the components, options trading is another, and advisory-service sentiment a third. In fact, the only indicator of the bunch that isn't based on contrary opinion is a cost-of-money gauge designed to show whether the Federal Reserve's monetary policy is "tight" or "easy."

Normally, the WSW Index fluctuates within a range of +5 (very bullish; buy) to −5 (very bearish; sell). Over the past decade, every +5 reading has resulted in gains of at least 20 percent for the stock market in less than a year. Similarly, every −5 reading has led to a serious decline (10 to 25 percent). To take a recent case, the WSW Index registered an extremely bearish −5 in June 1983, foreshadowing the painful pullback that followed over the next thirteen months. Then, in May and June 1984, the index shot up to a bullish +5. The market exploded in late July for a 16 percent gain on the Dow industrials in less than a month.

The safest strategy with the WSW Index is to buy mutual funds when the index hits −5 and hold them until the index rises to +5. This procedure should allow you to capture virtually all the profit that is to be made from a primary bull market. It is possible to trade the intermediate swings in the WSW Index (from −3 to +3, for example), but the risk of being whipsawed is much higher and you will probably end up paying more in short-term capital gains taxes than you will pocket in extra profits.

Selecting a Fund

Which funds to buy? Besides the gold funds, which are discussed separately in Chapter 9, I favor either the aggressive or the quality growth-

80

stock funds that sell their shares directly to the public without a sales charge (*load*). The aggressive funds, which invest heavily in technology stocks and other high-growth issues, are generally more volatile than the quality funds. Hence, they pose a greater risk to your portfolio if you fail to sell them close to the market's primary top. The quality funds are more forgiving and thus more appropriate for investors who don't follow the market on a day-to-day basis.

Table 5.1 provides details on several funds I recommend in both categories.

Buy and Hold?

Some investment theorists suggest that you can earn the best return from the stock market over the long pull by simply purchasing a mutual fund (or a portfolio of stocks) and forgetting about it. In fact, several mutual funds, called *index funds,* have been launched on this principle.

Table 5.1   **AGGRESSIVE GROWTH**

Fund	Minimum investment (initial/ subsequent)	Telephone switch?*	Change in fund value, 1/1/82 to 12/31/83† (percent)
Boston Company Special 1 Boston Place Boston, MA 02106 800-343-6324, 617-722-7250	$1000/none	Yes	88.2
Founders Special 3033 E. First Ave. Denver, CO 80206 800-525-2440, 303-394-4404	$250/$25	Yes	60.8
20th Century Select P.O. Box 200 Kansas City, MO 64141 816-531-5575	none/none	No	85.5
Vanguard Explorer P.O. Box 2600 Valley Forge, PA 19482 800-523-7025, 215-648-6000	$3000/$100	Yes	70.4

QUALITY GROWTH

Fund	Minimum investment (initial/ subsequent)	Telephone switch?*	Change in fund value, 1/1/82 to 12/31/83† (percent)
Mutual Shares 26 Broadway New York, NY 10004 800-221-7864, 212-908-4047	$1000/none	No	54.4
Guardian Mutual 342 Madison Ave. New York, NY 10173 212-850-8300	$200/$50	Yes	61.3
Windsor Fund P.O. Box 2600 Valley Forge, PA 19482 800-523-7025, 215-648-6000	$500/$50	Yes	57.0

*Shareholders may switch their investment to a money market fund by making a toll-free telephone call.
†Includes dividends and capital gains distributions.

These funds purchase an assortment of stocks that is designed to mimic a broad market index (such as the Standard & Poor's 500). Essentially, the fund's managers lock the shares away and swallow the key.

Many investors can tell charming stories about how well this type of long-term *buy-and-hold* strategy worked in the 1950s and 1960s. If you had bought almost any blue chip stock in the late 1940s—IBM, General Electric, General Motors, U.S. Steel—and had held it for the next twenty years, you would have racked up fabulous profits.

But the success of a buy-and-hold strategy seems to depend on the time frame you're looking at. Had you bought a portfolio of blue chip stocks in the summer of 1929, for example, it would have taken you twenty-five years to break even. Most people can't afford to wait that long to recoup their losses.

In these days of roller-coaster volatility for all markets, your survival as an investor may depend on your sense of timing. "Ripeness is all." If you plan to invest in the stock market, take a disciplined contrarian approach. Buy mutual funds and individual stocks when the odds are with you, when the sentiment indicators proclaim that the market as a whole is cheap. Sell when the odds of picking a winner are stacked against you, when the indicators warn that most of the bargains are gone.

Imitating the smart money (and going contrary to the market's perennial losers) may not sound like a heroic investment strategy, but it is common sense—and it works.

6
Bargains in the Wall Street Doghouse

But many that are first shall be last; and the last shall be first.

—Matt. 19:30

If Wall Street hates a stock, buy it.

—Martin Sosnoff

So you have decided that the market looks inviting. Stocks are cheap. What should you buy? A contrarian can take any of several approaches to stock selection, all of them equally valid and profitable. In essence, you should buy stocks that are out of favor—that nobody else wants. You should sell stocks that the Wall Street crowd has fallen in love with. But from that starting point, the road forks off in at least four directions. Let's explore the different routes.

The Growth Stock Strategy

If you follow the stock market closely and develop a strong sense of market timing, you might decide to invest in high technology or other volatile growth stocks—when the market as a whole is deeply depressed and investors are afraid to buy anything that seems risky. (Alternatively, you might buy shares of an aggressive-growth mutual fund that invests in these fast-moving growth companies.) When the market appears to be peaking, you can bail out and park your cash in Treasury bills or money market funds until the next major bottom draws near.

I have used this method with considerable success in my Individual Retirement Account (IRA), and I recommend it for active investors who

85

don't mind putting their portfolios through a major shakeup once or twice a year. If you invest in small- to medium-sized companies with fast-growing sales and earnings, you can make a lot of money in a relatively short time. But you must be prepared to concentrate most of your buying and selling within a couple of weeks (or days) near primary or intermediate bottoms and tops.

The rest of the time, this strategy requires you to summon up the iron discipline to do nothing. The glamour companies with the high price-earnings ratios are savagely unforgiving if you buy them too high or fail to sell them high enough. Altogether too often, they can fall even faster than they rose, a cruel but not unusual form of "capital punishment" for the investor whose timing was slightly off.

With a no-load mutual fund, the mechanics of buying and selling growth stocks are fairly easy, since many funds allow you to purchase or redeem your shares with a toll-free telephone call. However, because these stocks bounce around so much, you may feel compelled to switch into or out of the market several times a year, incurring heavy taxes on your short-term capital gains.* Furthermore, if you buy individual stocks, you will pay a king's ransom in brokerage commissions if you attempt to turn over your entire portfolio once or twice a year.

Accordingly, I recommend that you invest in growth stocks only if:

- *You don't mind watching the market on a daily basis,* and

- *You can accept sharp short-term fluctuations in the value of your shares.* It is much easier to be patient with volatile stocks if you restrict them to a fairly small percentage of your portfolio.

Moreover, you can probably improve your bottom-line results by a sizable margin if:

- *You limit your trading to no-load aggressive-growth mutual funds,* and

- *You shelter your short-term profits* in an IRA, Keogh plan, or other tax-deferred account.

*Under present law, if you make a profit on a stock you held six months or less, your short-term gain is taxed as "ordinary income" at rates up to 50 percent. Stocks held for more than six months qualify for favorable long-term capital gains treatment, with a maximum tax of 20 percent.

Since a mutual fund normally consists of fifty or more stocks in perhaps a dozen or more industries, you don't have to worry about diversification. Mathematical studies show that you need to own about fifteen to twenty-five stocks in at least half a dozen industries to protect yourself against the risk that some of your stocks may drop while most of the market is going up. Unless you can scrape together at least $10,000 to build a diversified stock portfolio, I heartily recommend that you go with no-load funds.

For investors who wish to choose individual growth stocks, one of the finest publications I have seen is Charles Allmon's newsletter, *Growth Stock Outlook* (P.O. Box 9911, Chevy Chase, MD 20815, $95 per year). Allmon, as crusty and contrary a character as you will find, has a superb record, stretching over two decades, for buying low and selling high.

"I wish he would name a couple of the IBMs, Xeroxes and Polaroids of tomorrow," you may be thinking. "Just let me buy some supergrowth companies and forget them." Unfortunately, as suggested in Chapter 5, I believe that a buy-and-hold-indefinitely strategy is dangerous in today's market environment, and especially dangerous with growth stocks. Figure 12 shows why you should view growth stocks as cyclical trading vehicles only, to be held during a primary bull market upswing—but no longer.

The graph plots the price-earnings ratio of the stocks in the T. Rowe Price New Horizons Fund (a typical aggressive-growth mutual fund) versus the price-earnings ratio of the broad market, as represented by the Standard & Poor's 500 index. (The *price-earnings* (P/E) ratio is simply the price of the stock, divided by the company's earnings per share.) You will notice that the P/E ratio for the New Horizons Fund in mid–1983 exceeded that of the S&P 500 by a factor of more than 2 to 1.

This awesome reading—the highest in the postwar era—indicates that growth stocks at the 1983 peak were more richly priced in relation to the rest of the market than at the frenzied speculative peaks of 1961, 1968, and 1972. In each case, when valuations got so far out of whack, a growth stock crash ensued, lasting at least two years.

Because the speculative mania for small, emerging growth companies has been building since 1977 (see Figure 12), it may take several years to unwind after the current primary bull market for stocks tops out. The carnage that took place in the high-flying over-the-counter market from June 1983 to mid–1984 was probably just a hint of what is coming. In the meantime, the contrary investor who is uncomfortable

New Horizons Fund P/E vs S&P 500

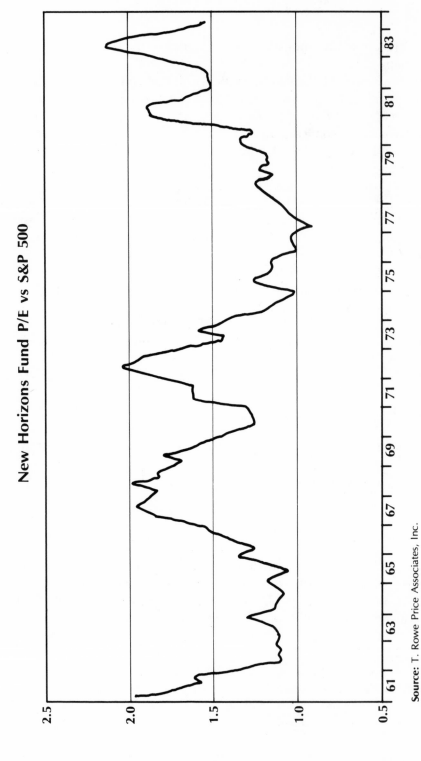

Source: T. Rowe Price Associates, Inc.

Fig. 12. New Horizons Fund

with the mounting risks in emerging growth companies will look elsewhere for authentic stock market bargains.

The Last Train to Dullsville

The second contrarian approach to investing in common stocks is to buy neglected, *dull* companies that the market has overlooked, or companies that have actually run into trouble (huge losses, bankruptcy, etc.). Ironically, some of the least desirable stocks in the market—the pariahs of Wall Street—are packed with the heftiest profit potential.

Common sense will tell you that a company that has fallen out of favor merely because it has done nothing exciting poses less risk than a company that is teetering on the edge of collapse. On the other hand, when a Lazarus-type stock rises from the dead (like Chrysler a few years back), it typically rolls up a much bigger profit for the patient investor. As a contrarian, you can choose from a broad spectrum of risk and reward.

Identifying dull companies is child's play. You simply turn to the stock pages of your local newspaper and look for companies with low price-earnings ratios (in the vicinity of 5 to 8). If most investors think a company's earnings are going to grow sluggishly, the stock will trade at a low price in relation to the company's current earnings per share. By contrast, if investors are confident that a company's profits are going to grow like gangbusters, they will bid up the price of the stock to a large multiple of the company's current earnings.

David Dreman's classic book, *Contrarian Investment Strategy*,[1] presented a barrage of evidence that, over the long pull, stocks with low price-earnings ratios dramatically outperform stocks with high multiples. The graph in Figure 13 adds further weight to his thesis. It shows the total return (dividends plus capital appreciation) provided by the 500 stocks in the Standard & Poor's 500 index over a twenty-year period from 1963 to 1982.

This graph breaks the S&P 500 down into quintiles (groups of 100 stocks), ranked according to their price-earnings ratios. As you can see, stocks in the lowest quintile brought the highest return (17.8 percent a year), while stocks in the three highest quintiles trailed the low P/E stocks by a country mile.

In late 1984, the price-earnings ratio for the broadly based Standard & Poor's 500 was about 10. (The index itself was approximately 167 in

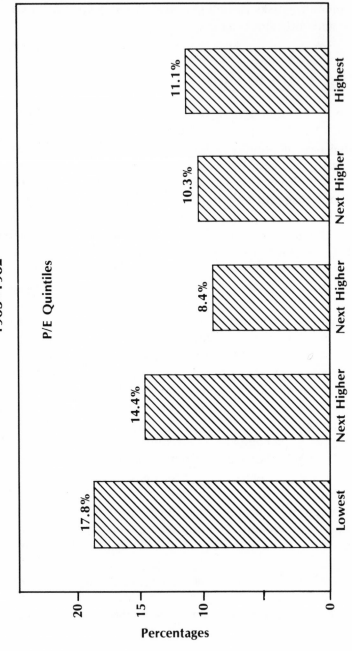

S.&P. "500"* Total Return
1963–1982

P/E Quintiles

17.8% Lowest

14.4% Next Higher

8.4% Next Higher

10.3% Next Higher

11.1% Highest

20
15
10
0

Percentages

Source: *Wall Street Transcript.*

*Unweighted for market capitalization.

Fig. 13.   S&P 500 total return

early November 1984.) Thus, any stock with a P/E in the 5 to 8 range would qualify as a bargain, assuming—as Dreman does—that the company's finances are reasonably solid (Dreman doesn't like distressed companies) and its accounting truthfully reflects current earnings.

Dreman recommends that you limit yourself to large, well-known companies that pay above-average dividend yields. (The average yield on the S&P 500 is currently 4.5 percent.) In addition, he favors companies that boast a higher rate of earnings growth than the S&P 500, both in the immediate past and projected into the near future. For simplicity, he suggests that you hold each stock in your portfolio until its P/E ratio approaches that of the market, and then replace it with a new low P/E selection.

It isn't necessary to buy stocks on the absolute bottom rung of the P/E ladder. In most studies, stocks in the second-lowest quintile have performed nearly as well as those in the bottom quintile, and have sometimes even beaten the bottom fifth. But if you are determined to buy the cheapest of the cheap, you can find a weekly listing of the 100 stocks with the lowest price-earnings ratios in the *Value Line Investment Survey* (711 Third Ave., New York, NY 10017, $365 a year, available in many public libraries).

Gaps in the Theory

Before you rush out and buy a Dullsville portfolio of low P/E stocks, however, let me offer a few caveats about the Dreman method:

• *Stocks in some industries can languish with low P/Es for years, or even decades.* A striking example is the international oil companies (Exxon, Mobil, Gulf, Texaco, etc.). These stocks as a group have traded below the P/E of the market *without interruption* since 1950! Even during the oil boom of the late 1970s, the international oils never came closer than a 10 percent discount to the price-earnings ratio of the Standard & Poor's 500.

After three decades of low P/Es, have the international oils outperformed the rest of the market? Under the Dreman thesis, you would expect them to. But consider Exxon, the bellwether of the group. According to the company's 1983 annual report, Exxon shares have netted investors a total return of about 9 percent annually in the twenty-five years since 1958—a negligible four-tenths of 1 percent above the overall market.

Banks are another example of an industry with chronically low P/Es. (Perhaps investors suspect that the banks have been reporting inflated earnings for a long time. Were Citibank's Latin American loans ever collectible?) Since 1975, the common stocks of most major banks have traded at a lower P/E than the market. Yet bank stocks have fared no better than the market averages.

• *Price-earnings ratios for cyclical stocks are often deceptive.* Certain industries like autos, steel, savings and loan, homebuilding (and home appliances), and stock brokerage make hay while the sun is shining. In times of prosperity, they report gigantic profits that drive the P/E ratios of their stocks down to tantalizing levels. (If earnings rise much faster than the stock price, the price-earnings ratio drops.) As soon as business turns sour, however, their profits plunge—along with their stocks.

Take a case in point: Ford Motor Co., a stock that Mr. Dreman recommended in the 1979 edition of his book.[2] At the time, Ford was trading at only three times earnings—a seemingly irresistible bargain. But the company and the auto industry were at a cyclical peak in their sales and earnings. By September 1981, a little over two years after Dreman's book was published, Ford stock had plunged 63 percent. Ironically, when Ford was a truly great buy (at the September 1981 lows), it had no earnings at all.

The low P/E theory gave a similar false signal in March 1981, when U.S. Steel was changing hands at only five times earnings. (As far as I know, Mr. Dreman didn't recommend U.S. Steel at the time.) Had you purchased this seeming bargain, you would have lost more than half of your investment within seventeen months. In fact, at a recent price of 28, the low P/E investor who bought U.S. Steel in 1981 is still sitting on a loss, despite one of the sharpest bull market rallies in history.

An even more recent example will ring a bell with thousands of unhappy investors. In June 1983, Merrill Lynch was selling for a P/E of 9—well below the P/E for the overall market (14). The brokerage industry was pumping out spectacular profits. Was Merrill a screaming buy? Well, the stock plunged 60 percent over the next eleven months as Merrill's earnings collapsed like an accordion.

I am not citing these unfortunate cases to discredit low P/E investing—far from it. Rather, I am bringing up this evidence to rebut the suggestion (by Dreman and others) that you can ignore the state of the general market when you select low P/E stocks. Market timing is vital! Ford Motor, U.S. Steel, and Merrill Lynch all registered low P/Es *close to important market peaks.* Had you been analyzing the broad market from a contrarian point of view, using the tools described in Chapter 5, you wouldn't have bought *any* stocks—high P/E or low P/E—at those treacherous junctures.

The time to buy stocks, whether they sport high or low price-earnings ratios, is after the market as a whole has fallen. Don't attempt to pick out bargains in a dangerously steamed-up market. There simply aren't any! Wait until the market has dropped and the contrary indicators are once again giving off bullish signals. Then, if you don't mind taking a businessman's risk, purchase the glamorous high P/E stocks (and aggressive funds). If you want less risk with possibly an even more generous long-term reward, buy the low P/E issues (and conservative mutual funds like the Windsor Fund).

Low P/E stocks will generally make money for you over the long haul even if your market timing isn't the sharpest. But there is no excuse for a contrary investor to chase stocks—even low P/E stocks—that have run up dramatically in a bull market. Wait for a good, painful setback before you buy. Given a little time, the market will nearly always accommodate you.

Utilities Light the Way

While it is impractical for me to recommend individual stocks in this book (since I don't know whether the market will seem cheap or dear when you read this page), I do want to call to your attention a low P/E *industry* that may have reached such an extreme level of undervaluation as to present a once-in-a-generation buying opportunity. I am referring to the electric utilities. Traditionally, most investors have purchased utility shares primarily for dividend income, and only secondarily for capital appreciation.

Nonetheless, my studies of industrywide P/E patterns lead me to believe that electric utility stocks may generate superior capital gains (compared with the market in general) as well as superior dividend yields in the years ahead. Figure 14 illustrates the basis of my argument. From 1952 to 1966—ancient times to most of today's investors—utility stocks traded at a higher price-earnings ratio than the market as a whole (the Standard & Poor's 500, in this case). In 1952, for example, the average utility P/E stood at a towering 40 percent premium to the market.

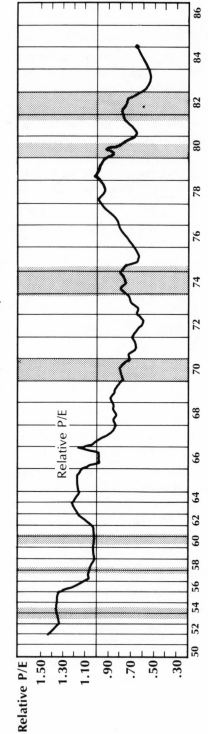

Electric Utility P/Es

Relative P/E

Relative P/E

Economic Cycles
Market Cycles

Source: A. G. Becker Paribas.

Fig. 14. Electric Utilities P/Es

94

Investors in the 1950s and 1960s thought of utilities as a growth industry. So boundless was Wall Street's enthusiasm for utility shares that in 1965, when the Dow Jones utility average made its all-time high, the average utility issue traded at a higher P/E than the average industrial stock. Incredible as it may seem today, the average utility stock sold for twenty times earnings. Some utilities in fast-growing service areas were even more richly priced: Texas Utilities had a P/E of 30 and Tampa Electric, 35—sky-high multiples that the market nowadays accords to only the most glamorous growth companies.

Once inflation began to take off in the late 1960s, the financial health of the utility industry deteriorated markedly. High interest rates, inflated construction costs, and inadequate rate relief dealt the industry a near-lethal blow. As a result, the price-earnings ratio of the average utility stock plummeted from a high of 22 in late 1961 to a low of 5.4 in the fall of 1974.

To be sure, P/Es for all stocks dropped during those years, but utility P/Es sank further—and stayed down. Since 1974, despite several primary bull markets for industrial shares, the average P/E for the Dow Jones utility average has never climbed more than fractionally above 8.

Even the huge market rally that began in 1982 hasn't lifted utility P/Es out of the dumps. As recently as May-June 1984, the P/E on the Dow utilities dipped to 5.8—within a whisker of the all-time low. Compared with the rest of the market, utilities at the 1984 lows were almost incredibly cheap; the industry's P/E was 45 percent below that of the S&P 500, the widest discount in history. Utilities were also returning more than twice the dividend yield of industrial stocks, the widest gap in history.

During the utilities' heyday in 1965, the yield on the Dow Jones utility average sank to 3 percent—*less* than the yield on the Dow industrials! Most utilities were selling back then for two or three times their book value per common share.* Today, most utilities are trading below book and some troubled nuclear companies are quoted at a minuscule 20 percent of book value.

Even though utility shares mounted a strong rally in the second

---

*A company's *book value* (also known as net asset value or stockholders' equity) is what is left of the company's assets after all its liabilities have been paid off. To put it another way: what the company *owns* minus what it *owes*. This is the portion of the company that belongs to the stockholders.

half of 1984, many are still selling for half to two-thirds of their 1965 prices. How many goods and services can you think of that cost less today than they did in 1965? Buying utility stocks at today's prices is comparable to paying $20,000 for a new house, $2000 for a new car, or $10 for a visit to the doctor.

Of course, the utility industry faces problems: soaring construction costs, high interest rates, sluggish growth in demand for electricity, punitive regulation. All these negatives are well known. What if, however—

- inflation winds down over the long term, after a worrisome uptick in 1985–86,
- interest rates ease (perhaps not immediately, but over a period of years),
- the economy grows faster than it did in the 1970s, stimulating consumption of electricity,
- oil prices remain steady, taking some of the urgency out of energy conservation, and
- the Reagan administration pushes through regulatory reforms to streamline the approval process for nuclear plants?

If all these "surprises"—or even just a few of them—come to pass, the utility industry could enjoy a renaissance. Indeed, the next fifteen years could prove to be the mirror image of 1965 to 1980. While I'm not predicting that happy outcome (I can't see fifteen years into the future), I suggest that you take this possibility into account by allocating a portion of your capital to utility shares.

In a stretched-out period of declining inflation, utility stocks would soar as dividend yields fell to compensate for lower long-term interest rates. Imagine, for example, that twenty-year Treasury bond yields dipped to $5\frac{1}{2}$ percent—the level that prevailed when Nixon beat McGovern in 1972. Utility stocks would likely double from today's prices, while paying you today's handsome dividends (together with any future increases).

Nukes: A Bargain Hunter's Dream

The contrary investor who is interested in utility stocks should ferret out those with the lowest P/Es. Almost invariably, this criterion will point you to utilities that are engaged (to some degree) in constructing nuclear power plants. Nuclear utilities offer a spectrum of risk to suit any taste. For low-risk investors who want generous current income as well as wide capital gains potential, I suggest strong, well-financed companies like New England Electric and Southern California Edison, both of which were yielding 9 percent in the fall of 1984.

If capital gains are uppermost in your mind, you should focus on companies like Arizona Public Service, Cleveland Electric Illuminating, Gulf States Utilities, Kansas City Power and Light, Middle South Utilities, Niagara Mohawk Power, and Union Electric. These utilities are carrying out ambitious, though by no means unmanageable, nuclear construction programs. All of the stocks were recently yielding 11 to 13 percent; the higher the yield, the greater the risk. My advice is to buy an equal dollar amount of all seven and use the dividends to purchase additional shares through the companies' automatic dividend reinvestment plans.

For the stunt drivers in the audience, who want all capital gains and no income (at least not currently), my favorite bombed-out nuclear utility has been *Long Island Lighting* (Lilco). This company has struggled for fifteen years to get its Shoreham nuclear plant on line. A cash crunch in early 1984 forced Lilco to omit its dividends, lay off 20 percent of its work force, and slash salaries for the rest. As a consequence, the stock crashed as low as $3^3/_4$—only a fifth of the company's book value per common share! If Lilco survives in its present form (and I think the odds are better than 50–50 that it will), I wouldn't be surprised to see the stock climb into the 20s within the next three or four years.

The best time to buy utility stocks is after interest rates have risen sharply for several months to a year. (Because power companies are continually issuing new stock to finance their construction budgets, prices of utility shares go down and dividend yields go up when interest rates rise.) A fine buying opportunity presented itself in mid–1984. However, the rally that followed in the second half of the year pushed the stocks up too far, too fast. Wait for the Dow Jones utility average to come down at least 10 percent from its 1985 highs before you plunge in.

Damsels in Distress

The Lilco story brings me to a contrarian's most cherished subject: distressed companies. *Distressed* doesn't necessarily mean *bankrupt,* though it can. Many fine companies with impressive long-term growth records go through troubled periods because of weak management, intransigent unions, regulatory harassment, and other factors.

Some of these unlucky firms drop into the dustbin of history, like W. T. Grant. Others pass through the purgatory of Chapter 11 and emerge in better shape than ever, like Penn Central. Still others—the most numerous group—manage, after a brush with disaster, to bounce back under a tough-minded chief executive (often a newcomer to the company). Chrysler is probably the most spectacular example of corporate back-from-the-brinkmanship in recent years.

The one feature that all distressed companies share is that their stocks crash—60, 70, 80, 90 percent, or more. Investing in bankrupt companies *after* their stocks have crashed can bring astonishing profits. Toys "Я" Us shares leaped thirty times in five years after the company emerged from bankruptcy in 1978. Penn Central, a more modest success, saw its stock quadruple in four years. However, each bankruptcy is unique, and it is often difficult to form an intelligent judgment about whether a bankrupt company will survive.[3]

Because bankruptcy presents so many legal and other complications, I think most investors who want to speculate in this area should work with an experienced professional adviser. As a rule, Wall Street firms that specialize in "bankruptcy arbitrage," as it is called, are tight-lipped about their activities and prefer not to deal with the public. However, Mutual Shares, a fund recommended in Chapter 5, has invested in bankrupt firms for more than thirty-five years, with outstanding results.

For most investors, the easiest, most straightforward approach to buying troubled companies is outlined by Lowell Miller in his book, *The Perfect Investment*.[4] Miller scans the stock tables to find companies whose shares have dropped to 20 percent or less of their previous five-year highs. His standard is somewhat less stringent for big companies and for stocks that have crashed despite an increase in earnings. If a stock was formerly valued in the market at more than $2 billion, for example, he will buy when the stock drops to 35 percent of the former high.

Utility stocks also qualify for the 35 percent cutoff, while banks must meet a 30 percent standard. If a company's earnings or dividends have increased from the former five-year high to the crash-point low, or if the company was valued in the market at over $1 billion and earnings have declined less than 25 percent from the high, Miller uses the 30 percent benchmark.

To screen out the dogs, Miller suggests a few other criteria:

- Generally, the stock, after its crash, should sell below book value per share.
- There must be "signs of life," such as dividends or earnings.
- Fad companies with obsolescent products should be avoided.
- The stock's price chart must show signs of an uptrend.

Miller also looks for *plus factors*, kickers that might indicate that the company is on the mend: a dividend reinstatement or increase, a low price-earnings ratio, insider purchases of the stock, a monopoly market for the company's products, and so on.

Miller maintains—and he has tables to prove it—that stocks selected according to these rules over the past decade have risen an average of 54 percent after one year, 84 percent after two, and 102 percent after three. In addition, more than 90 percent of the selections were profitable to some degree over all three time frames.

I can testify that his method works. In August 1982 (before Miller's book was written), I recommended Chrysler common stock and warrants to readers of *Personal Finance*. (A *warrant*, like an option, gives you the right to buy a stock at a fixed price for a specified time.) Although I hadn't heard of Miller at the time, my criteria were virtually identical to his: the stock had crashed, its book value was triple the market price, Lee Iacocca was putting on the hard sell, and the stock was moving up despite a powerful downdraft in the broad market. Chrysler turned out to be the best-performing stock I have ever selected (so far, anyway!), soaring 400 percent in ten months. The warrants jumped nearly ten times over the same period.

To keep up with Lowell Miller's damsels in distress, I suggest that you subscribe to his well-written newsletter, *Investment Values* (P.O. Box 517, Mt. Kisco, NY 10549, $80 per year). Recently, he has been stressing natural-resource stocks, many of which have plummeted 60 to 80 percent since 1980. Here are a few of his choices for the long pull and the prices at which he recommended them: AMAX ($23^{3}/_{4}$), Crown

Zellerbach ($32^1/_2$), DeKalb Agresearch ($24^1/_2$), Inexco Oil ($11^3/_4$), Standard Oil of Indiana (51), and Tiger International (7).

The Inside Scoop

You will recall that one of Lowell Miller's plus factors for a stock was insider buying. I would go a step further. I would argue that you can build a winning contrarian portfolio simply by purchasing stocks the insiders are buying, and selling stocks the insiders are selling—without doing any further research!

Of course, I am not suggesting that you should ignore the other factors that might draw your attention to a stock, a low P/E ratio, for example, or a Lowell Miller–style "crash." But if you lack the time or

Table 6.1   **INSIDER BUY SIGNALS**

Stock	Insider purchases/ sales in preceding 12 months	Price, 8/12/82	Price, 6/16/83	Gain, %
Pacific Lumber	9/0	$15^3/_8$	$28^1/_4$	83.7
Emery Air Freight	8/1	$8^1/_2$	$20^5/_8$	142.6
Planning Research	8/1	$5^3/_4$	$21^1/_8$	267.4
Baker International	7/0	19	$18^3/_8$	(3.3)
Bay Financial	7/0	$8^5/_8$	$15^3/_4$	82.6
Royal Crown Cos.	7/0	$15^5/_8$	$26^1/_2$	69.6
United Merchants	7/1	$4^7/_8$	$12^1/_4$	151.3
Handy & Harman	6/0	$12^7/_8$	$21^1/_4$	65.0
Tri-South Investments	6/1	$3^3/_4$	$6^3/_4$	80.0
Macmillan Inc.	5/0	13	$33^3/_4$	159.6
Average Gain				109.8
Gain for Dow Jones Industrials				60.7

the expertise to research stocks thoroughly, you can still make money by following the lead of the corporate insiders—America's most knowledgeable contrary investors.

In Chapter 5, I mentioned that stocks favored by insiders typically go up twice as fast as the market during a general rise, and that stocks dumped by the insiders go down twice as fast as the market during a general slide. Table 6.1 shows how this principle has worked recently, during the huge first leg of the bull market from August 1982 to June 1983, and during the long, agonizing pullback of June 1983 to July 1984.

Clearly, the insiders knew what they were doing! The stocks they liked best outperformed the Dow industrials by nearly a 2 to 1 spread,

Table 6.2   INSIDER SELL SIGNALS

Stock	Insider purchases/ sales in preceding 12 months	Price, 6/16/83	Price, 7/24/84	Loss, %
A.G. Edwards	4/35	$38^7/_8$	$19^7/_8$	(50.2)
Motorola	1/40	44.33*	$32^1/_4$	(27.3)
Digital Equipment	0/31	$113^1/_2$	$78^5/_8$	(30.7)
Control Data	0/27	$60^1/_2$	$24^5/_8$	(59.3)
Hilton Hotels	0/23	56	$46^3/_4$	(16.5)
Humana	1/22	32.81	$25^7/_8$	(21.2)
National Medical Enterprises	0/21	$30^3/_8$	$18^3/_8$	(39.5)
American Medical International	2/21	$34^3/_4$	$22^7/_8$	(34.2)
Wal-Mart Stores	2/19	$41^1/_8$	39	(5.2)
Lear Siegler	1/18	46	40	(13.0)
Average loss				(29.7)
Loss for Dow industrials				(13.0)

*Adjusted to reflect stock split.
Source: *The Insiders* (3471 N. Federal Hwy., Ft. Lauderdale, FL 33306, $100 per year).

while the stocks they deserted fell more than twice as far as the Dow when the market weakened.

Here are some basic rules for trading stocks with heavy insider activity:

- *Buy* when, marketwide, more insiders are buying than selling. Sell when insider sales exceed purchases by a 4 to 1 margin (higher in an extremely strong bull market).

- *Buy* an individual stock if three or more insiders buy the stock within a three-month period, or if the chairman (or president), and any other insider buy the stock within a three-month period.

- *Sell* a stock if four or more insiders sell within a three-month period. For technology companies and brokerage firms, raise the sell signal to six. But sell immediately, regardless of whether any other insiders are selling, if the chairman, president, or an outside director dumps a big block of stock (worth at least $500,000).

   In general, insiders sell more often than they buy because they acquire much of their stock at below-market prices through company stock-option plans. Such stock is really a form of deferred compensation—a bonus on top of the executive's paycheck. Often, the record shows, insiders sell their optioned stock without much regard to market value. Thus, it takes more insider sales to generate a sell signal than buys to generate a buy signal.

- If you get a mixture of buys and sells, go with the preponderance of insider transactions. Buy if buyers outnumber sellers by 3 to 1, and sell if sellers outnumber buyers 4 to 1. (See previous rules.) A transaction by the chairman or president counts as two votes on the buy side and three votes on the sell side.

Choose Your Weapons

Despite what some advocates for the theory of contrary opinion may say, there is no single, true-blue contrarian method for picking stocks. Some investors may prefer to buy glamour stocks after a sharp selloff. Others may favor stocks with low price-earnings ratios, while still others may adopt Lowell Miller's "perfect investment" strategy, which seeks to profit from stocks that have plummeted 70 or 80 percent. All investors can benefit from studying insider trading—and indeed, you can build a contrarian strategy on insider trading alone, if you wish.

Which method you should follow depends largely on your own tastes and preferences. If you are the patient, methodical sort, David Dreman's low P/E strategy will probably appeal to you. On the other hand, if you enjoy a good horse race, you might want to trade depressed glamour stocks or Lowell Miller's comeback candidates. Follow a strategy that makes you comfortable, or even several strategies if you want to experiment. For the contrarian, there is only one hard-and-fast rule of stock selection: *Don't buy what everybody else is buying.* If a stock is popular, the best profits are probably already sitting in someone else's pocket.

7
The Income Investor Fights Back

One thousand dollars left to earn interest at 8 percent a year will grow to $43 quadrillion in 400 years, but the first hundred years are the hardest.

— Sidney Homer,
A History of Interest Rates

For the past forty years, as well as for most of recorded history, investing for income has been a losing battle. If it were possible to amass a fortune by collecting interest and dividends, surely many of the ancient noble families of Europe, and even some of the old patrician families of America (the Adamses of Massachusetts, for example, and the Lees of Virginia) would long since have become "quadrillionaires."

Sad to say, what usually happens is just the opposite: great fortunes disintegrate, devoured by taxes, inflation, depression, regulation, war, revolution, expropriation, bad management, or simple waste. Even a small pool of savings can shrink drastically almost overnight, as some unlucky owners of Baldwin-United annuities or nuclear utility shares discovered in 1983–84.

In the fall of 1983, common stockholders of the Long Island Lighting Co. (Lilco) were earning a comfortable 11 percent dividend yield on their money. Ten months later, after demagogic local politicians "successfully" blocked the company's efforts to open its $4 billion Shoreham nuclear plant, the dividend had vanished and the value of Lilco stock had plunged 80 percent—an unsettling experience for the thousands of retirees who were relying on their Lilco checks to help meet living expenses. Governor Mario Cuomo, a Shoreham opponent known for his compassion, undoubtedly cried in his soup.

Government is, and always has been, the income investors' most implacable foe. It whittles down their earnings through taxation. Through inflation, it slashes the purchasing power of their interest and dividends. And, as Lilco shareholders learned to their dismay, the rampaging King Kong state may ruin a seemingly safe income-producing investment through heavy-handed regulation. To survive in this hostile environment, income investors must plan their moves carefully.

Forty Years of Rising Rates

While income investing is never profitable over the *very* long term (thirty, forty, or fifty years or more), this cloud, too, has a silver lining. As the British economist John Maynard Keynes said in one of his few indisputably true statements: "In the long run, we are all dead." The income investor doesn't need to worry about the long run. If you put your money in the right places for several years at a time, you can collect rich yields—and you may even enhance your real wealth along the way.

Today's income investor is fortunate to be living at a time when inflation has finally scared the financial markets out of their wits. Interest rates and inflation have been rising more or less steadily since the end of World War II (see Figure 15), but it has only been since 1979 that investors have demanded a sizable interest premium over the current inflation rate to compensate for the risk of higher inflation to come. For years, bond investors (to say nothing of the hapless millions who kept their savings in low-yielding bank accounts) earned little or nothing after inflation and taxes. Now, at last, the income investor is fighting back.

As I write, both short-term money market instruments (Treasury bills, for example) and long-term bonds are paying 5 to 8 percent *over the inflation rate* of the past twelve months. And those yields are only for top-quality paper—lower-rated merchandise is returning even more. Clearly, the rules of the game have changed.

Will these high *real* (inflation-adjusted) interest rates last indefinitely? Most money market analysts seem to think so. Their case rests on the belief that deregulation of the banking system (NOW accounts, money market savings accounts, market-rate CDs, etc.), has pushed interest rates to a permanently higher plateau. But as a contrarian, I

106

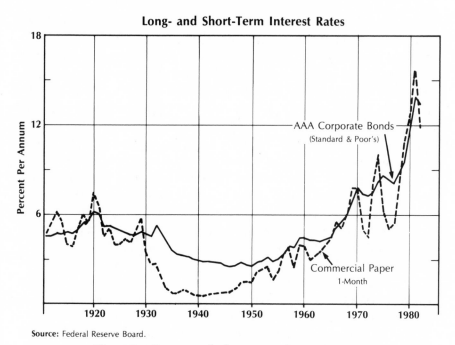

Long- and Short-Term Interest Rates

Source: Federal Reserve Board.

Fig. 15.   Long- and short-term interest rates

respect the wisdom of that early market sage, Heraclitus, who said: "There is nothing permanent but change."

Today's sky-high interest rates may, I think, be foreshadowing a financial crisis that could bring down the curtain on the postwar credit boom and, eventually, cause interest rates to collapse. For almost four decades—ever since long-term interest rates hit their lows of the century in 1946—government, business, and the consumer have been piling up debt at an accelerating pace, buying today and promising to pay tomorrow. Since 1950, the national debt has mushroomed from $260 billion to $1.5 trillion (six times), while business and household debt has risen even faster. Consumer or household debt, for instance, has multiplied more than thirty times!

While many economists shrug off these figures, the fact remains that the burden of servicing all this debt (paying the interest and principal as they fall due) has grown heavier and heavier with time. Interest on the national debt amounted to only 12 percent of the government's revenues in 1950, but 23 percent in 1984. One student of federal spending, R. Earl Hadady (editor of *Market Vane*), estimates that interest

107

payments will become the government's largest single expense before 1990 unless the federal deficit is slashed radically.

Consumers and businesses have gone even more deeply into hock than the federal government. Take a glance at Figure 16. It measures consumer installment debt—auto loans, credit-card balances, and the like, as a percentage of *disposable personal income,* a high-flown synonym for take-home pay. You can see that, since 1950, installment debt has more than doubled in relation to consumers' income. Likewise, mortgage debt has increased two-and-a-half times as a percentage of income. When you consider that interest rates on all this debt have gone through the roof, it becomes apparent that the consumer is carrying a heavier load of debt than ever before in America's history.

Corporations, too, have jumped into the act. Perhaps the most disturbing indication of how deeply businesses have indebted themselves is depicted in Figure 17. This graph plots corporations' liquid assets (cash and short-term interest-bearing securities like Treasury bills) as a percentage of short-term corporate liabilities. *Short-term liabilities* are debts a corporation must pay within a year.

As the liquid-asset ratio declines, a corporation has less and less

Household Debt Outstanding*

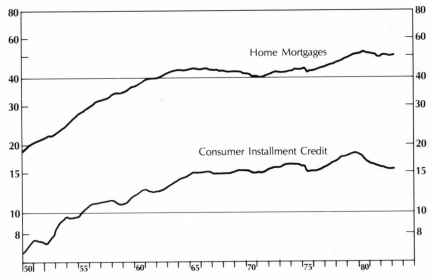

*As a percent of disposable personal income. **Source:** Federal Reserve Board.

Fig. 16.   Household debt outstanding

108

Corporate Liquidity Ratio*

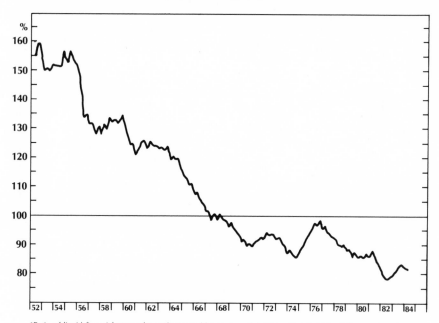

*Ratio of liquid financial assets plus trade receivables to current liabilities. **Source:** Federal Reserve Board.

Fig. 17.   Corporate liquidity ratio

flexibility to deal with unexpected reverses. In plain language, the firm is "strapped for cash." Figure 17 shows that, whereas U.S. corporations owned $1.60 of liquid assets for every dollar of short-term liabilities in 1952, holdings of liquid assets had plummeted to about 80 cents in 1984.

The banking industry, which is the financial nerve center of our economy, has gone through a similar liquidity squeeze. Figure 18 charts it. Since 1950, banks have been shoveling loan money out the door as fast as they dared, while running down their holdings of truly liquid assets: cash and investment securities. As a result, liquid assets today comprise only about 30 cents for each dollar of bank assets, versus 70 cents in 1950.

Since loans are much less liquid than cash or securities (you can't sell a loan instantly at face value), a bank that is thoroughly "loaned out" can run into serious problems with its depositors if even a small percentage of its loans go bad. Chicago's Continental Illinois Bank nearly failed in May 1984 because depositors panicked and wanted out. Yet only 7 percent of the bank's loans were classified as nonperforming.

109

Bank Liquidity

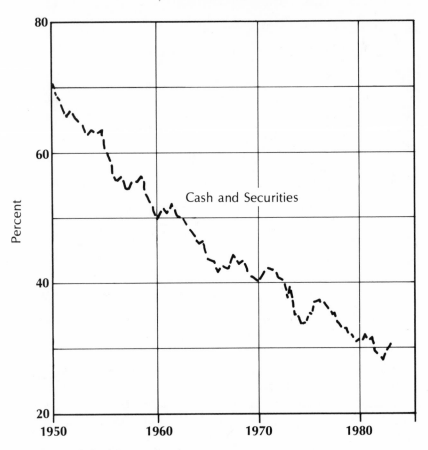

Source: Federal Reserve Board.

Fig. 18.   Bank liquidity

If the Continental Bank had fortified its balance sheet with cash and government securities, depositors would never have questioned the bank's soundness. But the depositors knew that Continental—like all major banks—was illiquid and overloaned. At a mere rumor of trouble, they turned tail and ran.

Credit Crunch Ahead?

Illiquidity—a shortage of cash to meet current obligations—is the hallmark of today's economy, whether you study the government sector, households, businesses, or banks. Decades of persistent inflation have convinced Americans that it makes more sense to buy now on credit than to save and buy later with cash. All of us have, to some degree, adopted a present-oriented perspective.

But how much more debt can we absorb? How much further can we allow our collective balance sheets to run down? Nobody knows precisely when we will reach the limit, but a few signs suggest that it may not lie too far ahead. For one thing, the Federal Reserve, as keeper of the nation's money supply, has been much more willing over the past five or six years to wage an aggressive fight against inflation. With the Reagan administration's tacit blessing, the Fed presided over a wrenching period of tight money in 1981–82, which, in the following year, resulted in the lowest inflation rate since 1965.

True, as argued in Chapter 8, the Fed's loose monetary policy, in the second half of 1982 and the first half of 1983, has probably ignited another cyclical wave of inflation that could crest sometime in 1985 or 1986. But the sharp run-up in interest rates during the spring of 1984 suggests to me that the money markets aren't going to give the Fed much room to inflate as the current cycle matures. Even with only a moderate credit tightening by the nation's central bank in the first half of 1984, the bond market virtually collapsed.

If the price of a typical bond can drop 25 percent in one year (May 1983 to May 1984) because of a modest credit-tightening move by the Fed, what do you suppose will happen if Mr. Volcker is forced to shut off the money spigot in 1985 or 1986 to combat a surge of inflation? My guess is that interest rates will soar and the economy will drop into another recession—possibly the recession that will break the back of inflation for the next fifteen or twenty years.

To be sure, this scenario is just a hunch, not a forecast. In a highly illiquid and volatile economy, it is impossible to predict how the debt crisis that has been building for the past four decades will be resolved. If the Fed (under pressure from the politicians) decides to bail out all the world's debtors, hyperinflation will result. More likely, though, the Fed will refuse to bail out more than a handful of essential institutions (like Continental Illinois). The authorities will inject enough money into these sick giants to prevent a wholesale deflationary bust, but not enough to fire up inflation in the grand old Richard Nixon–Jimmy Carter style.

In view of this nagging uncertainty, the most intelligent course for the contrary investor who wants to earn interest and dividends is to "hang loose." Everyone else is illiquid; therefore, you should do your utmost to put your investment portfolio and your personal affairs into a highly liquid position. Pay down your debts (including your home mortgage) and invest the bulk of your income-producing assets in short-term money market instruments. When the next credit crunch comes along, you will be sitting on *cash*—the asset that everyone else will want most. At that point, you will be able to snap up long-term bonds and similar fixed-rate investments for a song.

Bonds: For Speculators Only

Until the U.S. government proves that it can stop the inflation rate from bobbing up into double digits at the next cyclical peak, you should treat long-term bonds strictly as a short-term speculation. Bondholders have been repeatedly burned during the past forty years as rising inflation eroded the purchasing power of low-interest coupons while rising interest rates depressed the resale value of bonds. Someday, perhaps in the not-too-distant future, bonds will offer such high yields that prudent income investors will buy them and put them away for ten or twenty years, or more. So far, however, buying and holding bonds has been a loser's game.

In a stable economy with steady or declining interest rates, long-term bonds are a solid, conservative investment, providing twenty or thirty years of guaranteed interest payments. But in recent years, the tables have been turned: Bond prices have sometimes fluctuated more wildly than common stocks or precious metals! From May 1983 to May 1984, for example, the 8 percent bond represented by the Treasury bond futures contract on the Chicago Board of Trade plunged 25 percent—roughly twice as far as the Dow Jones industrial average and the price of gold dropped over the same time span, and almost as far as the highly speculative over-the-counter stocks.

The time to buy bonds for a cyclical speculation is at the height of a credit crunch, when interest rates are soaring and the newspapers are filled with excited reports about the mortal sickness of the bond market. In March 1980, for example, the *New York Times* published an article titled, "Living Without a Bond Market,"[1] which related how British industry has managed to get along without long-term fixed-rate financing. The implication was that the U.S. bond market was dying, too. To a contrarian, it should come as no surprise that the *Times* article coincided almost perfectly with a major bottom in the U.S. bond market (a major peak in interest rates).

The Market Vane commodity poll discussed in Chapter 4 can also give you a clue to important turning points in the bond market. Market Vane tracks advisory sentiment on Treasury bond futures, which serve as a reliable proxy for the bond market as a whole. When the bullish consensus on bonds drops below 20 percent, or averages in the low 20s for three or four weeks in a row, the bond market is probably close to a significant bottom. On the other hand, when the bullish consensus swells to 80 percent for several weeks in a row—as it did at the cyclical peak for bonds in May 1983—batten down the storm hatches!

If you plan to speculate in bonds at all, don't set too much store by the standard broker's advice—"Safety first." On the rare occasions when bonds present a good opportunity for capital gains, lower-quality (junk) bonds are nearly always a better bargain than their higher-rated counterparts.

During a credit crunch, investors begin to wonder whether the marginal bond issuers can continue to service their debt. The spread between the yield on high-grade obligations and lower-grade paper widens as prices for the junk issues drop more sharply.

Studies have shown that, even after you take into account the greater default rate for junk bonds, a diversified portfolio of lower-rated issues outperforms gilt-edged bonds over the long pull. However, I must emphasize the word *diversified*. If you can afford only a handful of different bonds, stick with Treasuries or other top-rated paper (corporates or municipals). Don't try to assemble your own junk bond portfolio consisting of three or four of "tomorrow's Chryslers." Just one lemon could throw you for an enormous loss.

Instead, if you want to own junk bonds, I recommend that you buy shares in a mutual fund that invests in lower-rated paper. Two well-managed junk bond funds are Fidelity High Income Fund (82 Devonshire St., Boston, MA 02109, 800-225-6190, 617-523-1919, minimum $2500) and American Investors Income Fund (P.O. Box 2500, Greenwich, CT 06830, 800-243-5353, 203-622-1600, minimum $400). Both were recently yielding over 13 percent. For investors in the upper tax brackets, Fidelity sponsors a High Yield Municipals Fund (minimum $2500), which yields about 10 percent tax free. All of these are no-load funds (no sales charge).

Closed-end funds are another type of bond fund to consider. These funds issue a fixed number of shares, which trade on a stock exchange or over the counter. You must buy or sell your shares through a stock-broker. (By contrast, open-end mutual funds like Fidelity deal directly with the public, continuously issuing and redeeming their shares at a price based on the value of the fund's portfolio.) Often, you will find that shares of a closed-end bond fund are selling at a discount to the fund's underlying assets. In effect, you can buy a dollar's worth of bonds for 90 cents or sometimes even less.

Closed-end bond funds usually perform about as well as the open-end funds, but yield slightly more because of the discount. As with the open-end funds, I prefer the lower-quality (higher-yielding) funds, which tend to move up faster in a bull market. Often, these funds also boast the deepest discounts. My recommended list includes John Hancock Income Securities (NYSE: JHS), Lincoln National Direct Placement Fund (NYSE: LND), State Mutual Securities (NYSE: SMS), and USLIFE Income Fund (NYSE: UIF).

Barron's publishes the discount (or premium) for the leading closed-end bond funds every week. At panic bottoms in the bond market, the discount usually widens, making these funds an especially attractive buy. In the spring of 1980, for instance, the discount on most closed-end bond funds was running about 20 percent, with some funds trading at as much as a 30 percent discount to their underlying assets. Later in the year, when the bond market rallied sharply, the discounts narrowed or vanished. Several of the funds racked up gains of 40 percent or more—on top of a 14 to 15 percent current yield!

Take a Ride in a Convertible

With convertible securities (bonds or preferred stocks), you can play the stock and bond markets at the same time. As the name implies, you can exchange a convertible bond or convertible preferred stock for shares of common stock at a stipulated ratio. Generally, a convertible yields less than a straight bond or preferred without the conversion feature. Because of this lower yield, prices for convertibles tend to be more volatile than bond or preferred stock prices.*

But since most convertibles yield more than their related common stocks, convertible prices also tend to be less volatile than common

*A preferred stock, unlike a common stock, pays a fixed quarterly dividend or, if it is an adjustable-rate preferred, a dividend tied to money market rates.

stock prices. Convertibles, in short, are tailor-made for the not-so-bold income investor who wants to participate in the stock market without assuming the full risk of owning common stocks. Moreover, if the stock market is going up in spite of a declining bond market (as in 1978–80), convertibles can appreciate while straight bonds are crashing.

Convertible bonds differ from convertible preferred stocks in several important respects. First of all, bonds are safer—from a legal standpoint, at least—than preferred stocks. A company is legally obligated to make interest payments on its bonds, but management has the discretion to reduce or omit dividend payments (even on preferred stock). In addition, if a company goes broke, bondholders receive their share of the company's assets before the preferred stockholders get anything. (The preferred stockholders, in turn, outrank the common stockholders.) Furthermore, a bond has a stated maturity date on which the issuer is obligated to pay the face value of the bond. Most preferred stocks don't feature a mandatory redemption date (though some do).

When choosing convertibles, a contrarian should begin by looking for industries and companies that have lost favor on Wall Street. If a company's stock is selling for a bargain price, chances are good that any related convertible security has also been battered down. In the spring of 1984, for example, many high tech and brokerage-house stocks were wallowing 50, 60, or even 70 percent below their 1983 highs. Likewise, their convertible securities had plummeted.

The Merrill Lynch $8^7/_8$ percent convertible bond, due in 2007, traded as low as $94^1/_2$ in May 1984, down from 181 less than a year before (a 48 percent decline). Any convertible that loses half its value in just eleven months deserves your serious attention! The Merrill bond would have brought you a 9 percent current yield while you waited for the stock to recover. You could also have picked up the Wang Laboratories $7^3/_4$ percent bonds due in 2008 for only 76, down 27 percent from the 1983 high. These bonds would have paid you a current yield of more than 10 percent, compared with less than a 1 percent dividend yield on Wang common stock.

Once you have pinpointed companies whose stocks look cheap on a contrarian basis, go to the *Standard & Poor's Bond Guide* or *Moody's Bond Record* to find out whether the companies you are interested in have issued convertible securities. These reference manuals, available in most public libraries, will spell out the conversion terms for each bond or preferred stock.

The most important number to know for any convertible is its *premium over conversion value*. This figure tells you how far the underlying common stock must rise before the convertible investor can make money by converting.

Let's take a hypothetical example to show how to calculate the premium: XYZ common stock, which pays no dividend, is selling for $20 a share. The company's 10 percent convertible bonds, which allow you to swap one bond for thirty shares of stock, are selling for 80 ($800 per bond). The bond's conversion value—the value of the stock you would receive if you converted the bond immediately—is $600 (thirty shares times $20 per share). Since the bonds are fetching $800 apiece, the premium over conversion value is 33 percent ($800 minus $600, divided by $600).

In most cases, it doesn't make sense to buy convertibles with huge premiums, 50 or 60 percent, for instance. As a rule of thumb, you shouldn't buy a convertible if the premium is greater than three times the difference between the yield on the convertible and the yield on the common stock. In other words, the extra income you earn from the convertible should erase the premium within three years.

For hard-money investors, I have occasionally recommended the Sunshine Mining Co. silver-indexed bonds, which are a form of convertible security. There are three issues, all due in 1995. The April and December maturities carry an $8\frac{1}{2}$ percent interest coupon; the February maturity, 8 percent. At the owner's option, each bond may be exchanged for 50 ounces of silver at maturity.

With these bonds, you can earn interest while hedging yourself against inflation. In effect, you are buying a bond coupled with an eleven-year call option on silver bullion. If silver skyrockets, you could exercise your call and swap the bond for metal. (Alternatively, you could sell the bond, since its price tends to go up—and down—with the price of silver.) But even if silver never sees $20 again, you still collect your interest.

Needless to say, you should consider the Sunshine bonds only when the price of silver is depressed. (See Chapter 8 for several indicators that will alert you to a bottom in silver.) In addition, I prefer to buy the Sunshines when they are trading at a discount to par value (less than 100 cents per dollar of face value). Remember, if silver languishes below $20 through 1995, the company won't pay you more than the par value of the bonds ($1000 apiece) at maturity.

Swelling the Income Stream

The major drawback to most bonds in an inflationary era is that their yields are fixed. Once you buy an ordinary bond, you receive the same semiannual interest payment until the bond matures, regardless of increases in the cost of living.

The income investor who wants to stay ahead of inflation can do two things. To begin with, if you own bonds (or any interest-bearing investment, including money market funds, and bank CDs), you should set aside a portion of your interest income to plow back into new income-producing investments. If, say, you are earning 13 percent a year on a $1000 Treasury bond and the inflation rate is 6 percent, you should reinvest at least $60 of the $130 of interest that you collect annually from Uncle Sam. If you spend more than $70 of your interest, you are eating into the purchasing power of your principal—a dangerous mistake—because, if you don't replenish your principal, the real value of your interest income will also dwindle as the years go by.

The second tactic you can employ is to invest in common stocks, real estate, and other assets that offer the prospect of a rising stream of income to combat inflation. In the last chapter, I recommended electric utility shares, especially the depressed nuclear utilities, for long-term capital gains. However, the more stable nukes also provide superb dividend yields in the neighborhood of 12 to 14 percent. With normal dividend increases, these yields could rise to 20 percent or more within the next five or six years.

Cleveland Electric, one of my favorite nukes for income, was recently paying better than 13 percent, and the company has raised its dividend every year since 1959. Arizona Public Service, which has upped its dividend annually since 1976, and Niagara Mohawk Power, which has boosted the payout each year since 1980, also qualify as good choices for income. For investors who put a premium on financial strength, New England Electric has raised its dividend every year since 1976 and Texas Utilities every year since—hold on to your seat!—1948, when the company was organized. But both of these companies yield less (under 10 percent) than the other nukes, though considerably more than non-nuclear utilities.

The near-collapse of the Continental Illinois Bank in the spring of 1984 revealed another group of high-yielding stocks that may appeal to the income investor: big "money center" (mostly New York) banks.

At the May 1984 lows, for instance, Manufacturers Hanover Corp. tumbled to half its 1983 high and was trading at a lowly three times the company's earnings per share.

Manny Hanny common was yielding over 12 percent, and the holding company for America's fourth-largest bank has increased its dividend every year since 1976. Since bank stocks usually bounce around more than utility shares, it is difficult for me to predict whether banks will rate a buy when you read this book. But if you are looking for stocks with high and rising dividends, you should investigate the big banks whenever talk of international loan defaults and other scary financial news stories reach the front pages of your local paper.

Big banks? Nuclear utilities? You are probably wondering why conservative, income-seeking investors would want to touch such "junk." The contrarian's answer, here as elsewhere, is: *The risk is less than meets the eye.* When the stock market—or any market—works itself into an emotional selling frenzy, prices usually drop so far that the balance between risk and reward tilts sharply in the buyer's favor. At a panic bottom, you can pick spectacular bargains out of the "junkpile." Next time the Chicken Littles of Wall Street tell you the sky is falling, ask if you can buy a piece.

Income Partnerships

Limited partnerships (LPs) can provide you with a rising flow of cash income, plus tax advantages to boot. The tax law allows a partnership, as distinguished from a corporation, to pass through to its owners all of the partnership's tax deductions. The partnership itself files no tax return; rather, the partners report their pro rata share of the partnership's income and deductions on their own individual returns.

In a limited partnership, the legal liability of the partners is limited to the value of the partnership's assets—if someone sues the partnership, for example. Most LPs are registered with the SEC, but some smaller partnerships (*private placements*) are not. Brokers can advertise the publicly registered partnerships, but not the private placements—you must approach the broker first. Minimum investment for public partnerships is typically $5000. For private placements, the minimum can range from $5000 to $100,000 (or even more).

Real estate and oil-and-gas are the two major areas in which syndicators have organized limited partnerships for income investors. Both sectors have taken investors for a rough ride over the past few years, fostering the current mood of caution and skepticism. Contrary investors are unperturbed, however, because they know that a depressed market is the only kind that is likely to go up and keep going up over the longer term.

In today's real estate market, you can expect an income partnership to pay out approximately 10 percent annually on your investment for the first few years, after which rising rents on the properties owned by the partnership may enhance your return. In many instances, the depreciation and other deductions make it possible for the partners to shelter more than half of their cash flow from current income tax.

Given the uncertain outlook for interest rates and the economy, I favor income partnerships that own their properties free and clear (with no mortgages). If you haven't got a mortgage, the bank can't foreclose! Several reputable partnership sponsors who adhere to this philosophy include:

- August Equity Partners (4401 Atlantic Ave., Suite 400, Long Beach, CA 90807, 800-821-3332, 213-428-8111). Pays cash to purchase "distressed" properties from overextended owners. $3000 minimum.

- E.F. Hutton (Insured Income Properties). Minimum lease income guaranteed by a major insurance company. Available through any Hutton office. A Hutton broker who has been helpful to *Personal Finance* subscribers is John J. Minahan (E.F. Hutton & Co., 3 New England Executive Park, Burlington, MA 01803, 800-225-5312, 617-229-8300). $5000 minimum.

- Realty Income Corp. (200 W. Grand Ave., Balcony A, Escondido, CA 92025, 800-854-1967, 619-741-2111). Invests for the very long term (fifteen years or more). $2000 minimum.

In the oil-and-gas area, I advise income investors to select partnerships that expect to derive most of their revenues from wells already in production, not merely under development. Because so many oil-partnership sponsors (most notably Petro-Lewis, which is one of the biggest) have run into financial trouble, I suggest that you put a premium on safety and go with Apache Petroleum Co., an income partnership listed on the New York Stock Exchange (ticker symbol: APP).

At a recent price of $17^1/_2$, Apache Pete was throwing off an 11 percent yield, completely free of current federal income tax. In fact, the part-

119

nership also generates tax deductions worth another 5 percent or so to an investor in the highest federal bracket. For instant liquidity, Apache Pete is unmatched. You can sell anytime, and your stockbroker can always quote you a current price.

In fact, liquidity is the major sore point with nearly all limited partnerships. Few sponsors maintain any kind of secondary (resale) market, so you should be prepared to sit with your LP until the general partner decides to liquidate—maybe six or eight years hence (or even longer). If you absolutely must liquidate early, perhaps because of a family emergency, I advise you to get in touch with a firm that specializes in repurchasing limited-partnership interests: the Liquidity Fund (1900 Powell St., Emeryville, CA 94608, 415-652-1462).

Your Rainy-Day Reserve

Stocks, bonds, and income partnerships can provide you with a rising, inflation-beating stream of cash. But the income investor who is trying to survive this era of illiquidity and uncertainty should also channel a hefty portion of his wealth into top-quality short-term instruments like Treasury bills, money market funds, and bank money market accounts.

I see nothing wrong with keeping 20 to 50 percent of your assets (not counting your home) in these liquid interest-bearing vehicles. They have easily outrun inflation in recent years, even after deducting the maximum federal income tax (50 percent). Liquidity (the ability to turn an asset into cash quickly, without loss of principal) is so scarce and so highly prized nowadays that the investor who has it can command handsome real (inflation-adjusted) rates of interest. In the fall of 1984, for example, three-month U.S. Treasury bills yielded as much as 10.6 percent, compared with an inflation rate of 4 percent.

As long as short-term interest rates remain well ahead of inflation, it will pay you to "keep liquid." A large chunk of cash and cash equivalents in your portfolio gives you the flexibility to deal with financial surprises that may overtake your family or the economy as a whole. In the bad old days of the 1970s, you had to accept a negative real interest rate—you were losing money after inflation and taxes—as the price for this insurance. Today, you can enjoy the security of money market assets while collecting a generous return that keeps you ahead of inflation and taxes. The income investor has found the next best thing to paradise!

For the ultimate in safety, you can buy Treasury bills directly from the government through your regional Federal Reserve Bank. (The Richmond Fed publishes a helpful booklet on the subject titled, "Buying Treasury Securities from Federal Reserve Banks." Write the Federal Reserve Bank of Richmond, P.O. Box 27622, Richmond, VA 23261.) The Treasury sells three-month and six-month bills every week, with a minimum face value of $10,000 (and $5000 increments thereafter). If you buy directly from the government, you avoid the commissions charged by banks and brokerage firms for purchasing Treasury bills. Also, since the Treasury holds the securities in your name, there is no chance that a bankruptcy court might seize your Treasury bill to pay creditors' claims if the bank or broker holding your bill should fail.

Treasury paper, purchased directly from the government or through a private bank or broker, is exempt from state income taxes on interest. In high-tax states like California, New York, or Massachusetts, this feature can make a big difference in your bottom-line return. Be sure to deduct your state income tax from any competing investment—like money market funds—when comparing Treasury bill yields with other short-term rates.

Money market mutual funds and bank money market deposit accounts (MMDAs) are vying eagerly for the saver's dollar. In most cases, money market funds offer a better return, although some banks, such as Citibank South Dakota (800-645-9181; in N.Y., 800-732-9636) and Chase Manhattan Bank USA (600 Market St., Wilmington, DE 19801, 800-245-1032), pay highly competitive yields. The minimum deposit to open an MMDA is $2500. You can write up to three checks per month against the account.

Most banks, however, don't bid aggressively for MMDAs. As a result, the typical bank MMDA yields considerably less—sometimes a full percentage point less—than the average money market fund. True, banks can boast $100,000 of FDIC insurance. But, as the Continental Illinois fiasco in May 1984 demonstrated, the federal government stands ready to guarantee the deposits of any large bank, regardless of the $100,000 limit.

Thus, money market funds that invest in certificates of deposit issued by major banks are probably just as safe as the banks themselves. If you still aren't sure, you can buy shares of a money market fund that invests exclusively in U.S. government securities. Here are three money market funds I recommend:

Capital Preservation Fund[2]
755 Page Mill Rd.
Palo Alto, CA 94304
800-4-SAFETY, 415-858-2400
$1000 minimum

Rowe Price Prime Reserve Fund
100 E. Pratt St.
Baltimore, MD 21202
800-638-5660, 301-547-2308
$1000 minimum

Scudder Cash Investment Trust
175 Federal St.
Boston, MA 02110
800-225-2470, 617-426-8300
$1000 minimum

With today's high interest rates, the income investor has a fighting chance to stay ahead of inflation and taxes. From time to time, in the aftermath of a credit crunch, long-term bonds can provide you with eye-popping yields as well as capital gains of 30 or even 40 percent in a single year. Nonetheless, because the inflation outlook is so uncertain and the credit system so unstable, you should favor dividend-paying common stocks, together with real estate or oil-and-gas partnerships, if you are seeking high current income. The rising cash payout from these vehicles will insulate you against inflation. It will also protect you to some extent from a sharp loss of principal if another credit crunch descends and interest rates skyrocket.

In any event, squirreling away an adequate liquid reserve in Treasury bills, money market funds, or the like is the beginning of financial wisdom. These instruments may seem boring, but in today's economy they maintain your purchasing power. Moreover, in a credit crunch, when cash is king, your rainy-day fund would enable you to scoop up bargains—stocks, bonds, real estate, whatever—that other investors might dearly love to buy but simply can't afford for lack of cash. A cash stash will save you in a crash!

8
Hard Assets: The Ultimate Inflation Hedge

Without gold we fold.
— slogan of the *American Gold News*

Show me an honest politician, and I will show you a society without inflation. *Inflation*, defined as an increase in the money supply that results in a general rise in prices, is a universal phenomenon, common to almost every organized society in every era—whatever the form of government. South Africa suffers from inflation, as does the Soviet Union. Inflation bedeviled the Roman Empire as much as the British. Kings and presidents may come and go, but the cost of living climbs relentlessly higher.

Of course, there have been interludes of falling prices. The United States experienced four months of net *deflation* in late 1982 and early 1983—the longest deflationary period in twenty-five years. Moreover, prices for some goods may decline in the face of inflation. (Computers and color TVs are cheaper today than they were ten years ago, for example.) But the long-term trend for most prices is always up, because most politicians—from Solon the Athenian to Tip O'Neill—prefer to pursue inflationary policies.

A little inflation is an appealing choice for politicians because it enables them to levy a hidden tax to finance their spending sprees. They need never vote on this tax or defend it to their constituents. To impose it, they merely spend money. If they spend more money than they can raise in visible taxes, they run a budget deficit, and borrow money (sell bonds) to pay the government's bills.

So far, no inflation. But when the government runs a massive budget deficit (as the United States did under Ronald Reagan in the early 1980s), the nation's central bank—our Federal Reserve—can do either of two things. Under the first alternative, the Fed can shrug its shoulders and let the Treasury sell its bonds and bills to the public at whatever interest rate the market may require to move the merchandise. However, since rising interest rates tend to depress economic activity (by increasing the cost of buying on credit), such a course would evoke shrieks of outrage from the politicians.

Instead, the Federal Reserve does what it knows the politicians want it to do: It buys some of the debt itself on the open market, paying for its purchases with money created out of thin air. This added demand tends to push prices up for Treasury bonds and bills, which is the same thing as lowering interest rates. The new money begins to percolate through the economy, driving prices up as more money chases the same quantity of goods. This, in simplified terms, is how the inflationary engine works.

Is Inflation Ending?

Some economic seers (such as A. Gary Shilling and Kiril Sokoloff, whose book is mentioned in Chapter 3), believe that the United States is headed for a long period of essentially stable prices with negligible inflation. Their argument sounded plausible enough in 1982 and 1983, when consumer prices edged up at less than a 4 percent annual rate. But by the summer of 1985, and perhaps sooner, I expect the "inflation is dead" thesis to have fallen by the wayside. Figure 19 explains why.

Years ago, Prof. Milton Friedman (formerly of the University of Chicago, and founder of the Chicago or monetarist school of economics) discovered that the U.S. inflation rate usually parallels the rate of growth in the basic M1 money supply eighteen to twenty-four months earlier. (M1, which consists of cash and checking accounts, represents readily available spending money.) This connection between money growth and inflation is one of the best-documented phenomena in economics. It is really just common sense: If you create money faster than you produce goods and services, prices rise.

As you can see from the chart, the Federal Reserve unleashed a

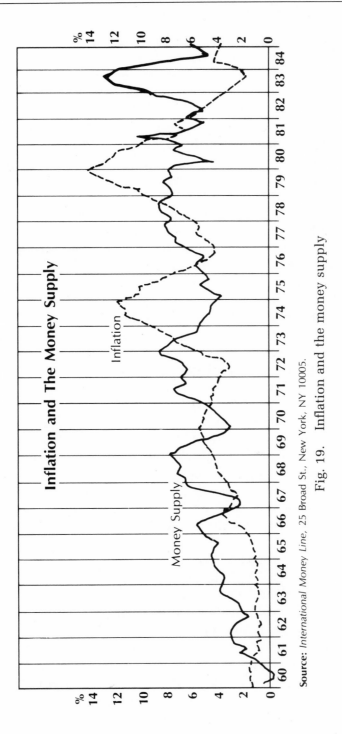

Fig. 19.   Inflation and the money supply

Source: *International Money Line*, 25 Broad St., New York, NY 10005.

torrent of "funny money" from mid–1982 to mid–1983. In fact, the year-to-year growth rate in M1 through July 1983 was the highest of the postwar era (13.6 percent). Many free-market economists protested this inflationary outburst, which the Fed engineered to gun the economy out of a recession. But the usual crowd of Keynesian (inflationist) pundits rushed to the Fed's defense, arguing that NOW accounts and other financial innovations had distorted the money figures.

Recent work by the Fed's own capable research staff suggests that any distortion in the M1 figures during 1982–83 was minimal, perhaps lowering the peak growth rate to 11 percent in July 1983, as opposed to 13.6 percent. No matter how you look at it, the Fed in 1982–83 promoted the most rapid twelve-month monetary expansion in this century. Double-digit money growth in 1983 implies that inflation will also creep back up in 1985, though perhaps not as high as 10 percent. Because the Fed did slow the growth of money dramatically during the last half of 1983 and through most of 1984, the next inflationary scare may not last beyond late 1985 or early 1986.

It is entirely possible that, from a long-term perspective, the U.S. inflation rate peaked in 1980. Inflation ebbs and flows with the business cycle, and the next cyclical high for inflation may fall short of the last one, just as each cyclical peak exceeded the previous one during the 1960s and 1970s (see Figure 19). In Chapter 6, I suggested that the price behavior of the electric utility shares may be foreshadowing a major break in America's long-term inflationary spiral.

However, even if the long-term "supertrend" of worsening inflation has reversed, the cyclical (two- to four-year) trend *is now calling for higher inflation.* When the inflation cycle is rising, you should arrange your portfolio to include a larger share of assets that will benefit from accelerating inflation. (I will talk more about portfolio building in Chapter 10.) When inflation is in a cyclical downtrend, you should stress investments that stand to benefit from slower inflation or even deflation.

Figure 19 shows that inflation apparently began a cyclical upswing in July 1983, when the growth rate of the Consumer Price Index hit bottom at 2.4 percent (year-over-year). Contrarians suspected that the inflation cycle was turning up because sages like the late Arnold Moskowitz (quoted in Chapter 3) were trumpeting that inflation was headed down to zero permanently. Accordingly, contrary investors at this stage of the cycle should be insulating their portfolios against inflation with hard assets like precious metals and mining shares, real estate, and perhaps even a few more exotic tangibles such as rare coins.

The Midas Metal

Gold has been the classic inflation hedge throughout history. Over the centuries, the "Midas metal" has retained its purchasing power while one paper currency after another has been thrown into the ash heap.[1] In the short term, however, the price of gold can fluctuate wildly.

The first rule of successful gold investing is to be skeptical of specific predictions about the price. To profit from a bull market in gold, you don't need to know whether the price two or three years from now will be $100, $1000, or $10,000 an ounce. As long as inflation is accelerating, gold will tend to advance. Similarly, once the inflation rate begins to slow, the price of gold will drop. Figure 20 makes the connection between gold and the inflation cycle abundantly clear.

My advice to investors who worry about the seemingly high price of gold ($300 an ounce today versus $35 in 1968) is: Study the mood of the market. Forget the fancy formulas and econometric models that

Fig. 20.   Gold and inflation

127

tell you how much gold (or anything else) *should* be selling for. If investors are overwhelmingly pessimistic about gold, as they were at the January 1985 lows, you should buy. And you should hang on to your gold until most investors are wildly enthusiastic about it, convinced that inflation will disappear. That frame of mind will mark the cyclical peak.

In Chapter 3, I suggested that you could identify major turning points in the inflation cycle and the price of gold by watching for enthusiastic predictions of zero inflation or even deflation by respectable advisers. In addition, best-selling books that prophesy either hyperinflation (at the top of the cycle) or deflation (at the bottom) can alert you to important turning points. On a more advanced level, I pointed out in Chapter 4 how the *Market Vane* poll can help you gauge investor sentiment in the gold market (or any other commodity market). Another contrary indicator that applies specifically to gold is depicted in Figure 21. Serious armchair analysts can track it every day in the *Wall Street Journal* or the *New York Times*.

The *gold call-put ratio* measures the mood of the speculators who buy gold futures options on the Commodity Exchange (Comex) in New York. (A Comex call option lets you *buy* a 100-ounce gold futures contract at a specified price within a stipulated time frame—a put lets you *sell* a contract under the same conditions.) Like options traders in other markets, the people who buy gold options on the Comex are trend followers with atrociously poor judgment. As the graph shows, they buy calls most heavily when the market is close to a peak, and they buy puts most heavily when the market is near bottom.

You calculate the gold call-put ratio by adding up the call volume (i.e., the number of calls purchased) over the ten most recent trading days and dividing it by the put volume over the same period. A speculator buys a call if he thinks the market is headed up, and a put if he thinks the market is headed down. Therefore, a high ratio of calls to puts (say, 3.0 or higher) implies that gold speculators are ravingly bullish. A low call-put ratio (say, 1.0 or lower) suggests that the speculators are snarlingly bearish. At these extremes, the majority is nearly always wrong. During a strong bull market, the call-put ratio will usually range from 2.0 to 3.0; in a powerful bear market, the ratio will normally drop into a range of 1.0 to 2.0.

The gold call-put ratio is a useful tool for contrarians who want to trade gold options and futures "against the crowd." (Several techniques

Gold call-put ratio

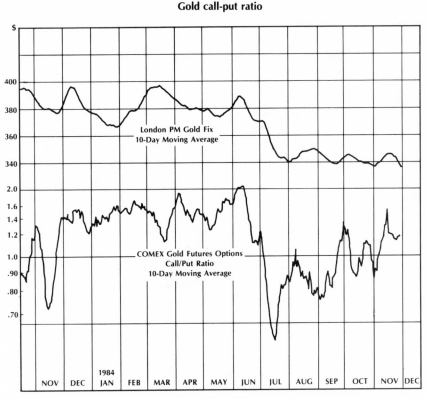

Fig. 21.   Gold call-put ratio

for making money with options and futures are described in Chapter 9.) However, I have found it equally valuable for timing purchases of physical bullion and mining shares. In January 1985, for example, the ten-day call-put ratio plunged to an incredible 0.581 as the price of gold bullion slipped to a five-year low (around $300).

Frenzied gold bears were buying five puts for every three calls—a truly amazing statistic when you consider that most options traders are by nature optimistic (why else would they play such a high-risk loser's game?). In virtually every options market, speculators purchase many more calls than puts. This burst of pessimism provided convincing evidence that gold and gold stocks were close to rock bottom.

The call-put ratio also warns of trouble at the top. In January and February 1983, it fairly shouted that the gold market was dangerously overbought. It also pointed to trouble in August 1983, when for a couple

129

of days the ratio soared above 4.3. Sure enough, the price of gold took another plunge, from the $420 area in August to $363 the following January.

As with most sentiment indicators, it is often difficult to tell immediately whether the gold call-put ratio is signaling a change in the market's primary trend or simply an intermediate correction against the primary trend. But in general, *the more extreme the reading, the more severe the reaction is likely to be.*

After the turn has occurred, you can judge whether it was of long-term or only intermediate-term significance. If, for instance, the market has been weak for months but a sickly rally pushes the call-put ratio way up (signaling too much optimism), look out for a sharp, nerve-jarring relapse. Beware of any market move that attracts too many followers too quickly. On the other hand, if the market climbs sharply *without* attracting a flood of call buying, prices may be able to keep climbing. A bull market must climb a wall of worry.

By the same token, a bear market must slide down a chute of over-confidence. If the call-put ratio (or any other sentiment indicator) shows that investors are quickly turning pessimistic whenever prices dip, the primary uptrend will likely resume. But if overconfident investors keep buying calls as prices drop, the market will probably drop further and a primary downtrend is under way.

How to Buy Bullion

Owning gold is easy nowadays. For people who want to buy their gold and their stocks from the same source, many Wall Street brokerage firms offer accumulation plans. One of the best is Merrill Lynch's Share-builder Plan (P.O. Box 520, New York, NY 10008, 800-221-2856), which allows you to start a gold or silver account for as little as $100. Commissions are low, especially for purchases of $1000 or more. You can sell your holding anytime with a toll-free telephone call.

Personally, however, I prefer to keep my gold close by (in a bank safe-deposit box), just in case I need to get at it in a hurry. At the moment, it seems unlikely that the government would try to confiscate private gold again. But if Washington panicked during a financial crisis, who knows what crack-brained legislation might result? By keeping your metal near at hand (I don't recommend home storage because of the security problem), you give yourself an added measure of flexibility.

If you plan to take physical possession of your gold, I suggest that you purchase bullion coins (coins that sell for close to their bullion value) such as the South African Krugerrand, the Canadian Maple Leaf, or the Austrian 100 Coronas. The Krugerrand and the Maple Leaf contain exactly 1 ounce of pure gold, but I favor the 100 Coronas (despite its odd weight of .9802 ounces of fine gold) because it generally trades at a lower premium over melt value.

For small investors who don't care to fork over $300 for a single coin, my favorite small piece is the handsome and historic British sovereign, which contains just under a quarter-ounce of pure gold (.2354 oz.). In early 1985, sovereigns were retailing for about $75. I would buy sovereigns whenever the retail price is no more than 10 percent above the coin's bullion value. For the larger, 1-ounce bullion coins, a 5 to 6 percent markup is usual.

Choosing a reputable coin dealer is crucial. In recent years, investors have lost hundreds of millions of dollars by ordering gold and silver from boiler-room outfits that had no intention of delivering the merchandise. Several well-established firms that I recommend for their quality service and low markups are: James U. Blanchard & Co. (4425 W. Napoleon, Metairie, LA 70001, 800-535-7633, 504-456-9034), Liberty Coin Service (300 Frandor Ave., Lansing, MI 48912, 800-321-1542, 517-351-4720), and Republic Bullion (1605 W. Olympic Blvd., Los Angeles, CA 90015, 800-762-4653, 213-381-5578, affiliated with Republic National Bank of New York).

If the threat of confiscation really bothers you, you might consider storing your gold with a firm outside the United States. You could open a bullion account with a Swiss bank. Or, if your taste is somewhat less exotic, I recommend Canada's Guardian Trust Co. (74 Victoria St., Toronto, Ont. M5C 2A5, 416-863-1100), which issues certificates representing metal in storage. Minimum purchase is 5 ounces of gold, but for silver, the minimum is 250 ounces. Guardian, a publicly traded company, has been in business for more than fifty years and is one of Canada's most highly regarded bullion dealers.

Silver: The Restless Metal

Silver in the past five years has been much more volatile than gold. For example, during the last six months of 1979 and the first month of 1980, the price of gold tripled. But the price of silver soared six times.

Likewise, in the 1980–82 crash, gold fell "only" 65 percent, while silver plummeted 90 percent. Since the June 1982 lows for both metals, silver has continued to experience wider price swings than gold.

Because of its volatility, I think silver is suitable primarily for investors who have already amassed some gold and want to diversify into a faster-paced market. Silver will give you all the excitement you are looking for—and more.

While I buy silver mainly with the idea of selling it later at a profit, some people stockpile bags of circulated "junk" U.S. silver coins, minted before 1965, as long-term insurance against a monetary crisis. In the event of a nuclear war, a worldwide banking collapse, or some other unforeseen economic catastrophe, old U.S. silver coins—dimes, quarters, and half dollars—might take the place of checkbook money and credit cards in small retail transactions (at the grocery store, for example, or the gas station).

This isn't the kind of risk I lie awake at night worrying about. However, I respect the market judgment of the people who buy bags of junk coins. These long-term investors know how to recognize value. As good contrarians, they consistently buy low and sell high. In fact, their activity in the marketplace provides a reliable indicator of where the price of silver is headed. I call it the "junk silver barometer."

As a rule, bags of circulated silver coins trade at a premium to the melt value of the silver. For instance, a dealer might sell a bag of coins with $1000 face value for $8000. At the same time, if the coins were melted for their silver, they might fetch only $7150. In this case, junk silver would be selling at a 12 percent premium to melt value ($8000 minus $7150, divided by $7000).

To compute the melt value of a bag, you simply multiply the spot price of silver (the cost of immediately deliverable warehouse silver on the commodity exchanges) by the number of ounces of silver in a bag (715). In the example above, I assumed that the spot price of silver was $10 an ounce. If you multiply $10 by 715, you get $7150—the melt value of the bag in our example.

Many reasons have been advanced to explain why junk silver trades at premium over melt value: Silver coins are scarcer than silver ingots (only a fixed number of coins were minted), it costs more for dealers to handle bags of small coins rather than large bars or ingots, and so on. Whatever the reason for the premium, the interesting fact for investors is that the premium rises, in contrary style, when the spot price

132

of silver falls. By the same token, the premium drops when the price of silver rises.

Apparently, the conservative, long-term investors who dominate the junk silver market tend to buy more heavily when the market is low—at the same time the nervous speculators who dominate the futures market are driving down the spot price with their selling. Thus, the spot price falls faster than the price of junk silver, boosting the premium for junk silver.

The opposite phenomenon seems to occur when the market is high: The conservative investors tend to pull back from buying junk silver (they may even liquidate on balance), while the speculators drive up the spot price of silver with their frenzied buying. The premium for junk silver shrinks.

Figure 22 shows how the junk silver barometer has behaved since 1982. At the major cyclical low for silver in June 1982, the premium soared to 56 percent—the highest level on record. At $5 an ounce, silver was deeply depressed. In real terms (inflation-adjusted dollars), the metal was selling at its lowest price in a decade. Silver promptly tripled over the next eight months.

If you study the chart, you will notice that the premium for junk silver fell rapidly in the last quarter of 1982 as silver prices shot up. At the intermediate peak in February 1983, the premium had all but vanished: With silver at nearly $15 an ounce, the junk silver barometer read a lowly 1 percent. The market was ready to crash—and it did.

Silver made another intermediate peak in August-September 1983. Once again, the premium on junk silver shrank to a minuscule 1 percent. The market dutifully took another steep tumble. Unfortunately for silver investors, the premium never opened up to more than 28 percent in 1984, even though the price of silver plunged to less than $6 an ounce. Apparently, conservative investors were unconvinced that silver had hit a solid bottom. Hence, they were unwilling to bid aggressively for bags of junk coins.

Here are a few basic rules for buying and selling silver with the barometer:

- When the barometer moves sharply in one direction for several weeks at a time, the silver market is approaching a turning point of at least intermediate-term significance. A sharp rise in the

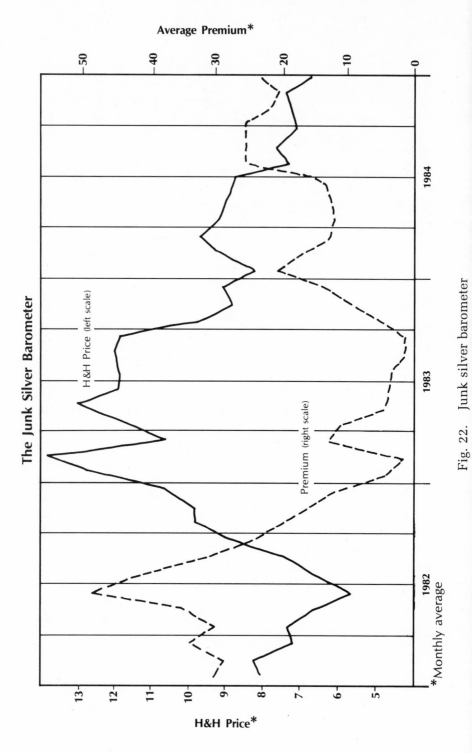

Fig. 22. Junk silver barometer

premium suggests an approaching bottom; a sharp drop implies that the market is peaking.

- A climactic move of 6 to 10 percentage points on the barometer in the space of a week often marks the exact turning point.

- A primary bear market for silver isn't likely to end until the barometer climbs to at least 30 percent, and perhaps higher.

- A zero premium is a strong warning that the market is about to drop sharply. If the barometer goes to a discount, as it did at the manic peak in January 1980, you should get out of silver and stay out until the inevitable crash has run its course.

For investors who wish to buy physical silver, I recommend the certificate storage programs of Citibank (399 Park Ave., New York, NY 10043, 800-223-1080) and Benham Certified Metals (755 Page Mill Rd., Palo Alto, CA 94304, 800-447-GOLD), as well as the Merrill Lynch Sharebuilder Account. Minimum investment for Citibank and Benham is $1000. An interesting feature of the Citibank program is that you can pay for your metal on your Visa card. There is no carrying charge if you pay when you receive your next Visa statement.

Because of the premium, I generally don't recommend junk silver coins except as a survival holding. Silver bars nearly always sell at a lower premium over melt value (typically 6 to 10 percent at retail).

Mining Stocks: Your Own Grubstake

Besides bullion, the metals investor can buy shares of gold- and silver-mining companies. Most of the time, mining stocks travel in the same direction as the underlying bullion. But the relative performance of the two vehicles can vary considerably over the short term.

Sometimes bullion acts stronger than the shares; sometimes vice versa. Over the long run, however, as in the past ten years or so, bullion and the mining shares have followed more or less parallel tracks. During the first phase of the primary bull market that began in June 1982, the mining shares ran way ahead of bullion (both silver and gold). In fact, South African gold stocks in the fall of 1984 were more costly in relation to bullion than they have ever been.

But at some point, given the historical pattern, it is reasonable to expect that the market will correct this imbalance: Either the mining shares will fall faster than bullion, or bullion will rise faster than the shares. Since my analysis suggests that a primary bull market for inflation and the metals is under way, I would expect bullion to outperform the shares as the cycle matures. But as long as the stock market is trending higher, it may continue to give a lift to the mining shares. Thus, their abnormal strength versus that of bullion could persist for a while longer.

Mining shares are a pretty homogeneous group. Silver stocks generally move in the same direction as gold stocks, though not necessarily at the same pace. (Gold shares in the past decade have been more volatile.) Moreover, individual shares within each of the two categories usually show similar gains or losses. The exception is the *junior* companies, notably the exploratory *penny* mining shares (those selling for less than $1), which typically rise further in a bull market than the major mines do—and fall further in a bear market.

Since mining shares normally go up or down together, I would advise most investors not to hunt for "the big winners." It simply isn't worth the effort. Instead, the easiest and, I believe, most profitable strategy is to buy a widely diversified portfolio of shares when the mood of the market is gloomy, and gold and silver stocks are cheap. Sell off chunks of your portfolio when the crowd is enthusiastic about the mining shares, and prices are high.

I have already described several contrary indicators that will tell you when gold and silver bullion are undervalued or overvalued. Most of the time, these signals work equally well for the mining shares. If you plan to invest in gold shares, however, you might keep an eye on another indicator that is specifically designed to measure investor sentiment in the share market: the *ASA put-call ratio*. You can compute this ratio in three minutes every week by referring to the options pages of *Barron's*.

ASA Ltd. is a closed-end investment company that holds a diversified portfolio of South African gold shares. Since it is a closed-end fund, it doesn't continuously issue new shares and redeem old ones, as a mutual fund does. Instead, ASA has a fixed number of shares outstanding, which trade on the New York Stock Exchange. Call and put options on ASA stock are listed on the American Stock Exchange. Because of its diversified portfolio, ASA acts as a bellwether for the gold shares as a group.

Essentially, the ASA put-call ratio is based on the same idea as the other call-put ratios I have discussed: When options speculators are buying *puts* as if there were no tomorrow, the market is usually close to a bottom. When they are buying *calls* at a frantic clip, the market is generally near a top. Paul Eldridge, technical analyst for Howard Ruff's *Financial Success Report*, discovered the ASA indicator, and I track it regularly for readers of *Personal Finance*.

Figure 23 demonstrates the remarkable correlation between the put-call ratio and the price of ASA stock (or gold stocks generally). Whenever the ratio climbs above 0.8, the mining shares are approaching a good intermediate bottom, while a reading above 1.2 is likely to mark a major or primary bottom—the type you see every five or six years. Likewise, a dip below 0.5 on the put-call ratio is likely to spell big trouble for the gold shares, on either an intermediate- or a long-term basis.

To calculate the ratio, you add up the week's volume in ASA put options (as reported by *Barron's*) and divide it by the call volume. Since the weekly readings are often erratic, I keep a five-week moving average to smooth out the series.

Earlier, I noted that a diversified portfolio of mining shares makes far more sense than trying to pick a few "superstocks." Some of the established North American gold producers, which I think offer better value than the South Africans, include Agnico-Eagle (OTC: AEAGF),

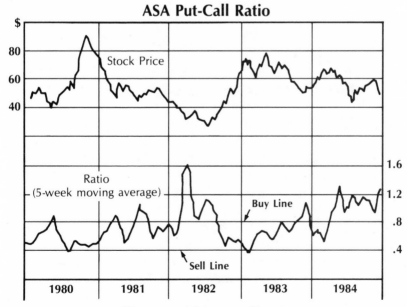

Fig. 23.   ASA put-call ratio

137

Campbell Red Lake (NYSE: CRK), Echo Bay (ASE: ECO), Giant Yellowknife (ASE: GYK), Malartic Hygrade (ASE: MHG), and Pegasus Gold (OTC: PGULF). I would avoid buying ASA itself, unless the stock is trading at a 20 percent or greater discount to the fund's net asset value. You can check the premium or discount weekly in *Barron's* or the Monday edition of the *Wall Street Journal*.

For most investors, though, I think the wisest choice is to buy into a no-load mutual fund like United Services Gold Shares (P.O. Box 29467, San Antonio, TX 78229, 800-531-5777, 512-696-1234) or its companion Prospector Fund, which invests *exclusively* in North American mines. Minimum investment for either fund is only $500. You can buy or sell these funds via a toll-free telephone call at the fund's closing net asset value each day. Prospector Fund, established in 1983, is too new to have much of a track record, but U.S. Gold Shares has consistently outperformed ASA stock over the long haul.

Unfortunately, there are at present no mutual funds devoted exclusively to silver-mining shares. If you are interested in silver stocks, you can form a basic portfolio by purchasing equal dollar amounts of Callahan Mining, Coeur d'Alene Mines, and Hecla Mining, three leading producers. Speculators who would like to play the penny gold-and-silver shares should work with a broker who keeps close tabs on this wild and woolly market. I recommend Jerry Pogue of National Securities Corp. (500 Union St., Seattle, WA 98101, 800-426-1608, 206-622-7200). Minimum account, $3000.

Real Estate: Success from Distress

While precious metals and mining shares aren't the only hard assets you can buy to hedge yourself against inflation, they are certainly the most liquid. You can sell them quickly, anytime, without having to make drastic price concessions. Nonetheless, the theory of contrary opinion applies to any market, including the less-liquid tangibles like real estate, rare coins, gemstones, art, and antiques.

Real estate is doubtless the most widely owned of the hard assets. It also tends to show the most stable appreciation—at least during periods of moderate inflation. When rapidly accelerating inflation leads to soaring interest rates and a credit crunch, however, real estate speculators can get burned—as Florida condominium developers (and their banks) discovered in the 1973–75 recession, and as thousands of California homeowners were reminded during the 1979–82 recession.

For the contrarian real estate investor, many of the finest buying opportunities emerge during (and after) a credit crunch. In the residential sector, skyrocketing interest rates make it expensive for builders to carry an inventory of unsold homes. At the same time, lofty mortgage rates scare buyers away, putting pressure on builders to slash prices through rebates, below-market financing, or other gimmicks.

The recession that follows a credit crunch may also force deeply indebted apartment owners to sell their properties at distress prices as young renters move back into their parents' homes and apartment vacancy rates surge. Likewise, corporate bankruptcies, layoffs, and a general cost-cutting drive by businesses may push office vacancies up and rents down, severely crimping landlords' cash flow. Office developers who mortgaged to the hilt during the boom can no longer meet their interest payments. They must sell, at almost any price.[2]

The real estate market isn't a monolith: Prices for single-family housing can chug along while those for office buildings are crashing, for example. One city can experience rising apartment vacancies while shortages of rental housing prevail in another city within the same state. But you can usually spot an important bottom for real estate prices in your area by the following criteria:

- *News reports focusing on the distressed real estate industry.* You will read and hear about unemployed construction workers, builder bankruptcies, real estate agents looking for second careers, soaring mortgage delinquencies, and the unaffordability of housing at current interest rates.

- *Housing starts at or near a multiyear low.* Often, housing prices remain flat or continue to drop even after housing starts begin to turn up. If you find a pattern of low housing starts, stable-to-lower prices, and rapidly falling interest rates, jump in! The bear market is probably ending.

- *High vacancy rates* for apartments or office buildings in the area, as compared with previous years.

- *A peak in the local unemployment rate,* followed by a month or two of declines. If people are out of work or afraid of losing their jobs, they aren't going to bid aggressively for real estate. Hence, prices are likely to be low.

- *Uncommonly courteous real estate brokers.* This is a subjective indicator, but nevertheless one of the best. When brokers have plenty of time on their hands, they tend to be less pushy and more eager to please. They will pamper you. They won't rush you to sign on the dotted line. Real estate investing is much more enjoyable under such circumstances.

The opposite characteristics signal a top:

- *Glowing news reports about the booming real estate market,* perhaps tempered by worries about rising mortgage rates.
- *A peak in housing starts* (or permits issued by your local building inspector), followed by several declines. This is a powerful warning.
- *Low vacancy rates in apartments and office buildings,* sparking a construction spree. When you see a construction crew working on every vacant lot in town, you should think about selling.
- *A multiyear low for the local unemployment rate,* followed by two or three seemingly innocuous upticks.
- *Rude, hard-nosed brokers.* A favorite broker's line at the top of the market (it was used on me in 1979 when I was looking for my first house) is: "If you don't buy now, you'll never be able to afford a home again." Brokers don't want to bother with browsers at the peak of the boom, they want to pile up commissions fast. The universal hard sell will tip you off that the market is about to go bust.

For many people, a major drawback to investing in real estate is the amount of capital required. Limited partnerships, which pool the resources of many individuals, can erase or at least mitigate this disadvantage. Although there are, no doubt, many contrarian real estate syndicators throughout the country, one I know and recommend is J. W. English Real Estate Inc. (P.O. Box 487, Walnut Creek, CA 94596, 800-423-8423, 415-838-8100).

The principal of this firm is Dr. John Wesley English, author of *The Coming Real Estate Crash,* which correctly predicted the collapse of the real estate boom in the late 1970s.[3] Wes is currently organizing partnerships to acquire distressed apartment buildings in Houston. He is an outstanding negotiator. In one case, he persuaded a desperate seller to *pay him* $79,000 to take an apartment building off the owner's hands—better than a "nothing down" deal! Minimum investment for Wes English's partnerships is typically $30,000.

If you want to buy and manage your own distressed properties, you can probably find candidates in your area by scanning newspaper advertisements and talking with local banks. Just make sure you pay 20 to 50 percent below appraised value. If the present owner wants to get rid of the property badly enough to accept a discount in that range, do him the favor.

Collectibles and Other Tangibles

In recent years, many Americans have invested in collectibles—including art, antiques, rare coins, rare stamps, and gemstones—as a hedge against inflation. While these assets have risen fabulously in value over the long term, they pose some serious disadvantages for the investor who isn't prepared to hold them for at least five to ten years because you buy at retail and sell at wholesale prices. The spread between the price you pay to buy and what a dealer pays you when you sell is enormous. Dealer markup typically comprises 30 to 50 percent of the retail price.

Fine differences of quality, which may be noticeable only to a trained eye, can make a dramatic difference in price. This is especially true with rare coins and gemstones. Unless you are willing to become an expert yourself, you must rely on experts to grade your merchandise for you. Unfortunately, most dealer-experts tend to grade loosely when selling *to* you but oh-so-strictly when buying *from* you!

Despite these disadvantages, collectibles can rack up stunning gains for the patient investor who is prepared to buy and hold for at least three to five years, and preferably longer. Rare coins, in particular, have performed superbly over the decades. The numismatic market is also the most highly developed of all the collectible markets, with the largest number of auctions, and even a dealer teletype network that provides current price quotations.

The most important rule a contrarian should observe when investing in rare coins (or any collectible) is: *Avoid fads.* Buy quality items that have attracted a steady following of collectors over the years, but don't buy *anything* when it is "hot." In the spring of 1984, for example, many coin dealers were touting U.S. $20 gold pieces of the St. Gaudens design (1907 to 1933) as a device for sidestepping the new IRS regulation that requires dealers to report your name when you sell gold bullion. My mailbox was crammed with advertising flyers making this pitch.

The $20 St. Gaudens is, of course, a staple of the numismatic market with a long history of upward price movement. But the promotional hype pushed the price of the St. Gaudens double eagle far out of line with other U.S. gold coins—all of which were equally exempt from the IRS reporting requirements. The same week that I warned *Personal Finance* readers about this absurdity, the "Saints" began to fall. Within seven months, they had plunged 30 percent.

If you plan to invest in rare coins, I suggest that you work with a low-pressure dealer like R. W. Bradford, proprietor of Liberty Coin Service (300 Frandor Ave., Lansing, MI 48912, 800-321-1542, 517-351-4720). Bill Bradford has a remarkable eye for bargains, and he *hates* fads. Buy the classic U.S. coins when the market is quiet and dull and sell them when stockbrokers and other self-styled "financial planners" start peddling them to a greedy and gullible public.

As long as high and volatile rates of inflation remain a part of the economic landscape, hard assets—from gold and silver to real estate and Chagall lithographs—will belong in the prudent investor's portfolio. Nobody can say (yet) whether the climax of America's long-term inflation problem was reached in 1980, or whether we face another, still greater crisis. But a cyclical surge of inflation is almost certainly under way. To cope with the threat of a shrinking dollar, the shrewd contrarian will buy inflation hedges while the crowd still believes that inflation is dead. When the public wakes up, finds that it has been deceived, and tries to protect itself by rushing into hard assets—it will be time to sell.

9
More Bang for the Buck

Give me a place to stand, and I will move the world.
—Archimedes on leverage

Not everyone is cut out to be a speculator. Some people just don't like to take big risks and would prefer to earn a modest payback on their investments rather than throw themselves open to the possibility of a major loss. Others, especially people in their later years, can't afford to speculate. If they squander their savings on ill-advised ventures, time may never give them an opportunity to make up their losses. Retired people, as a rule, should concentrate on preserving their wealth rather than multiplying it through high-risk enterprises.

In previous chapters, I argued that some types of assets that conventional wisdom regards as speculative really aren't nearly as risky as they may appear to be at first glance (nuclear utilities or junk bonds, for instance). In this chapter, however, I will discuss several techniques that only the diehard speculator—the compulsive high roller—will want to try. If you don't fit into that category, pass on to Chapter 10, or read what follows for entertainment only!

All of the speculative vehicles I describe in this chapter exploit the principle of leverage. In simple terms, *leverage* means making money with other people's money. The speculator puts up a small amount of money, which he or she can afford to lose entirely, in hopes of making a much larger profit. Buying stocks and bonds on margin (or selling them short) is probably the oldest and most familiar form of leveraged speculation. More recent inventions include warrants, options, and futures contracts.

Some contrarian advisers deplore what they see as a dangerous trend toward speculation in this country. In a recent issue of his newsletter, Donald J. Hoppe, an incisive practitioner of contrary thinking, warned: "For the past decade, the greatest speculative mania in history has been building up, and it has now reached that point of complete irrationality which typically precedes a major crash." Hoppe went on to observe:

The popular idea now is that every kind of hedge strategy must be employed against every contingency, and that no possibility for speculative profit should be overlooked. Above all, one must be continually active in as many markets as possible and employ leverage to a maximum degree. These popular notions are typical of the final stages of a speculation mania, when almost everyone is consumed by greed and is more concerned with missing opportunities for big profits than protecting their capital.[1]

While Hoppe may be slightly overstating the case, it is certainly true that the inflation of the past ten years or so has bred a get-rich-quick attitude in many investors. Many fear that unless they take extraordinary risks (in hopes of snaring gargantuan returns), inflation will destroy their chances of accumulating wealth. Indeed, millions of people are speculating without even knowing it—homebuyers who sign up for adjustable-rate mortgages (ARMs), for example. If interest rates skyrocket, these unlucky homebuyers could see their mortgage bills escalate by thousands of dollars a year—a potentially crushing blow to many a family's finances.

The burgeoning of the options and futures markets over the past ten years is also a mixed blessing. Inflation and a topsy-turvy economy have created a genuine need for institutional investors to hedge themselves against wildly seesawing stock and bond prices. Likewise, metals dealers, grain dealers, and other commercial interests have looked to the futures markets for protection against gyrating commodity prices.

But futures and options also attract hordes of naive speculators who dream of making a fortune—fast. It is entirely possible, as Donald Hoppe suggests, that the boom in leveraged speculations really does foreshadow the last days of a financial era—and the approaching "Big Bust" that deflation seers have prophesied for so long. But I think it is a mistake to advise *everyone*, under all circumstances, to avoid these instruments. As a matter of fact, if a crash is coming, investors may not be able to preserve the value of their capital except through short selling and other aggressive tactics. By observing a few basic rules, contrarian speculators can greatly reduce their risks and increase their odds of making sizable profits.

The Ten Commandments of Speculation

Here are ten principles you should follow if you plan to venture into the exciting world of leveraged speculation. Most of them aren't original with me. I am especially indebted to Charles Stahl, veteran gold trader and editor of *Green's Commodity Market Comments,* who laid down many of these rules for speculators at the annual Contrary Opinion Forum in Vermont back in 1967:

1. *Speculate with money you can afford to lose.* If you are trading with money that you know you will need next month for a down payment on a new house, or next year for your child's college tuition, emotions will cloud your judgment. Make sure you have set aside an adequate liquid reserve to pay for life's necessities before you attempt to speculate.

2. *Always keep more than the broker's required margin on deposit in your account.* When you buy securities on margin, trade commodity futures, or "write" (sell) options, you must deposit a minimum amount of money (*margin*), with your broker to assure that you will meet your obligations. Never deposit only the minimum margin, because a relatively small market movement against you could wipe out your stake. With commodity futures, put up at least twice the required margin and preferably more.

3. *Limit your losses.* Determine in advance how much risk you are willing to bear. When you enter a transaction, give your broker a standing order to *offset* (close out) your position if your losses reach a predetermined point. It is essential to set loss limits *in advance* because, if the market goes against you, you will cook up a multitude of excuses to convince yourself that you should hold on in the face of mounting losses. Accept losses gracefully. As long as you don't lose more than a predetermined amount of money, a time will come for another try.

4. *Never speculate if your personal life is in disarray.* If your wife

is sick or your teenage son is in trouble with the police, the paranoia and self-doubt that bedevil risk takers will torment you even more. Controlling your emotions is crucial to success as a speculator.

5. *Don't play every horse.* Most of the time, most markets aren't going anywhere. There simply aren't any big profits to be made. Resist the temptation to "keep your money working" on some speculation, somewhere, all the time. In most markets, good buying or selling opportunities come no more than once or twice a year. The rest of the time, you should put your idle funds into Treasury bills or other money market instruments, sit back, and count your interest.

6. *Undertrade.* This rule is a corollary of the Second and Fifth Commandments. Once you have decided how much of your capital you want to set aside for speculation, don't commit more than a portion of it to any single trade. If, for instance, you have allocated $5000 to buying options, don't buy more than $1500 worth of options at any time. If you see an interesting opportunity that would bring your total exposure to more than a third of your capital available for speculation, get rid of one or more existing positions before you enter the new trade.

7. *Fear the market.* When a speculation begins to show a profit, many people relax and complacently assume that the profit will last. Too often it doesn't. The market reverses itself and pretty soon the speculator is taking another loss. As soon as your speculation moves into the profit column, enter a standing order with your broker to sell (or cover your short sale) if the price slips back to your entry point. If your profits keep expanding, move the stop order up (a *trailing stop*) to protect your hard-won gains.

8. *Don't worship charts.* Many technical analysts claim to see critical *support* levels and *resistance* levels on price charts. (If the market previously made an important reversal at a certain price level, that price theoretically becomes support if the reversal was from down to up, and resistance if the reversal was from up to down.) Supposedly, the odds are better than 50–50 that prices will not drop below a support level or rise above a resistance level. If prices do break through these imaginary barriers, technicians say, the market is likely to keep going in the direction of the breakthrough.

However, there is absolutely no scientific evidence that any market pays attention to support or resistance levels. In fact, the growing popularity of technical analysis in recent years has had a perverse effect: When prices break through an assumed technical support or resistance level, the market often turns on a dime, whipsawing the unfortunate souls who believed the chart gazers' gospel. Apparently, savvy traders who see the market approaching the magic number place their bets that the price will break through. This buying (or selling) becomes a self-fulfilling prophecy. Then, when the price does break through the supposed barrier, the same traders jump to the opposite side of the market and prices snap back.

Needless to say, you can also write off the fancy patterns that technicians often think they see on their charts: head-and-shoulders formations, wedges, pennants, islands, saucers, Vs, Ws, parabolas, and the rest. These patterns may tell you how vivid an imagination the chartist has, but don't bet your bank account on them! You can safely draw only two conclusions from reading a chart. If the price is going up, something good must be happening to the underlying asset. If the price is going down, something bad must be happening.

Since charts merely record historical prices, it is impossible to judge, from chart reading alone, whether the good news or bad news will continue, any more than you can drive a car by staring into the rear-view mirror.

9. *When you make a profit, withdraw half of it.* The speculator who executes a successful trade is sorely tempted to pyramid his or her profits—to reinvest all the profits in a new speculation. The danger, though, is that a severe loss on the second trade may wipe out the gains on the first. Whenever you roll up a nice profit on a trade, withdraw half of the gain and put it out of harm's way, in Treasury bills or a similar safe, interest-bearing vehicle.

10. *Resist the impulses of the crowd.* In other words, think like a contrarian. Don't chase markets that have run up sharply, or sell markets short that have been collapsing for some time. Any profits you might make from following the existing trend are likely to be insignificant, and the risk of a painful reversal is high.

The Magic of Margin Accounts

A margin account with your stockbroker can greatly enhance your profits from trading stocks and bonds—if you are prepared to follow the Ten Commandments of Speculation. When you *buy on margin*, you deposit a down payment with your broker and he lends you money to purchase securities.

The interest rate the broker charges you on the margin loan floats up and down with the rate he pays to borrow from the bank (the *broker loan rate* or *call money rate*). At most full-service brokerage firms, the margin rate is close to the bank prime rate, but some discount brokers make margin loans for a point or more below prime. You can keep the loan as long as you want—brokers don't fix any repayment schedule. The interest is added to your debit balance daily. However, you must always maintain a large enough margin deposit in the account to satisfy your broker that the loan is safe.

The Federal Reserve Board, which regulates broker loans, currently requires you to put up an initial margin deposit equal to at least 50 percent of the purchase price of any stocks you buy on credit. If the value of the stocks in the account drops, your broker may send you a *margin call*, demanding that you deposit more margin to secure the loan. On the other hand, if the value of the stocks goes up, you can draw funds out of the account as long as you meet the broker's minimum *maintenance margin*.

Let's look at the arithmetic of a margin purchase to see how you can leverage your profits. We will assume that you bought 100 shares of XYZ stock at $20 a share, and that the margin rate stayed at a steady 12 percent for one year. You deposited the minimum 50 percent margin and borrowed the rest of the purchase price from your broker. At the end of a year, XYZ stock was trading at $40 per share. Table 9.1 shows how your profit from a margin purchase would compare with your profit from a straight cash purchase.

Table 9.1 PROFIT COMPARISON

		Cash Purchase	Margin Purchase
(a)	Proceeds of sale	$4000	$4000
(b)	Cost of stock	$2000	$2000
(c)	Net profit	$2000	$2000
(d)	Initial cash outlay	$2000	$1000
(e)	Interest expense	0	120
(f)	Total cash outlay	$2000	$1120
(g)	Percent of profit on total cash outlay (c/f)	100%	178%*

*A taxpayer in the 50 percent bracket who itemized deductions could have recovered half of the $120 interest expense on his or her tax return. Thus, the true cash outlay would have been only $1060 and the profit 189 percent.

148

When a stock rises sharply, the speculator who puts up 50 percent margin can earn almost twice as much profit as the more conservative investor who buys for cash. But interest expense always puts a drag on a margin account. In our example, unless XYZ stock gains at least 12 percent within a year (disregarding the tax benefit of deductible interest), you would have been better off to buy the stock for cash. Furthermore, leverage can work in reverse: With a 50 percent margin account, your losses pile up twice as fast (compared with a cash account) if the stock drops.

Because of today's historically high interest rates, I generally don't recommend buying stocks on margin. There are better ways to leverage your stock market profits, and some of these alternative methods— writing put and call options, for example—allow you to *collect* money rather than paying it out.

Margin buying makes much more sense with bonds. First of all, the leverage is greater: You need only deposit 30 percent of the purchase price when you buy corporate bonds on margin, and as little as 10 percent when you buy Treasury bonds. However, I don't recommend that you buy anything on 10 percent margin, not even real estate, and especially not bonds. A 10 percent drop in prices—two such instances occurred in 1983–84—would wipe out your margin deposit.

The beauty of buying bonds on margin is that bonds nowadays pay a generous rate of interest, offsetting the interest you owe on your margin loan. When long-term bonds are really worth buying as a cyclical speculation, they pay a higher interest rate than the margin-loan rate, which is tied to short-term money market rates. Hence, you make money on the spread between long-term and short-term rates, much as a bank does by borrowing short and lending long.

Never buy bonds on margin when the yield curve is inverted— when short-term money costs more than long-term money. But if, after a panic selloff in the bond market, you find that short rates have dropped below long rates, buying bonds on margin can reap spectacular profits. From June 1982 to May 1983, for example, you could have rolled up a total return (interest plus capital gains) of 260 percent on your money if you had purchased long-term Treasury bonds on 10 percent margin!

Selling Short—and Avoiding the Pitfalls

Probably the most valuable use of a margin account is for selling short. A short seller is a speculator who is trying to make a profit from a drop, rather than a rise, in the market. Most investors, and many brokers, are afraid to sell short because theoretically, the losses from an ill-considered short sale can mount to infinity. When you sell a stock short, you sell shares that you don't actually own. Instead, you borrow the stock from your broker and sell it.

Naturally, you hope to replace the borrowed stock (cover the short) later at a lower price than you received when you sold. For a short seller, the lower a stock goes, the better. If the stock drops all the way to zero, you earn your maximum profit—100 percent. But if the stock rises instead, you will lose money when you cover your short. In theory, the stock could keep going up forever, and you would have to buy back the shares at an infinitely high price. Novice speculators often balk at short selling because the risk-reward ratio seems unfair—an infinite risk versus a maximum reward of 100 percent. Moreover, Uncle Sam taxes any profits you earn from a short sale as a short-term capital gain (ordinary income), regardless of when you cover your short.

However, short selling isn't as risky or unprofitable as it appears at first blush—if you respect the Ten Commandments of Speculation. To begin with, no stock soars to infinity, and if you sell short when the market is bubbling with euphoria after a sharp runup, the odds of a major decline vastly outweigh the likelihood that the market will stage another dramatic advance.

Furthermore, you don't need to pay any margin interest on a short sale (because you are borrowing stock, not money). If you wish, you can put up interest-bearing securities such as Treasury bills as collateral for your short sale, thereby avoiding any cash outlay. For short sales of stock, the cash margin requirement is 50 percent of the value of the stock sold short. However, if you put up securities as collateral, the market value of the securities must equal the value of the stock you are selling short.

Once you have decided that the market looks vulnerable, selecting stocks to sell short isn't especially difficult. As veteran short seller T. J. Holt is fond of saying, "Short the overpriced favorites." As a rule, the stocks that rise the most during a bull market—the stocks the crowd loves best—fall the most during a bear market. Here are some characteristics that flag a stock as a good short-sale candidate:

- Price earnings ratio twice or three times the market average
- Minuscule dividend yield (or none at all)
- Price gains far in excess of the market indexes over the past twelve months
- Heavy insider selling (preferably one or more transactions worth $500,000 apiece)
- Company or its industry featured on the front cover of a national newsmagazine
- Company's product (often a fad item or vanity product) attracting intense competition and profit margins beginning to sag

Most of the stocks that came down hardest during the collapse of the 1983 speculative mania shared these characteristics. Apple Computer, Coleco, Mary Kay Cosmetics, Mattel, Osborne Computer, Warner Communications—hundreds of glamorous stocks with P/Es of 20, 30, or more crashed. For the legions who thought that over-the-counter growth stocks could only go up, up, up, it was a hair-raising toboggan ride. Short sellers, on the other hand, loved every minute of it.

The New World of Options

Options trading has exploded in recent years, almost to the point of becoming a mania. You can now buy or sell (write) options on more than 300 stocks (and a variety of stock indexes), as well as bonds, gold, silver, and foreign currencies.[2] A call option gives you the right (but not the obligation) to buy a certain quantity of an asset—say, 100 shares of stock—at a fixed price (the strike price) during a specified period. Speculators buy calls when they expect the price of the underlying asset to go up.

A put option allows you to sell a given quantity of the underlying asset (again, perhaps 100 shares of stock) at a fixed price during a specified period. Speculators buy puts to profit from a decline in the market.

The appeal of options lies in their enormous leverage. When you buy an option, the price you pay (the premium) is usually a small fraction of the value of the underlying asset. For example, if Sears Roebuck stock is trading at $30 per share, you might be able to buy a call option, entitling you to purchase 100 shares at 30 within the next

151

three months, for only $2 per share. If Sears stock gained only six dollars within the next three months—a 20 percent rise—the owner of the call would triple his or her money.

You may wonder how I reached that breathtaking conclusion. Let's briefly study the arithmetic. You agreed to pay $2 per share for the option. To triple your money, the option must appreciate to at least $6 by the expiration date. If Sears stock is at 30 or *below* on the expiration date, your call option will expire worthless. It wouldn't make any sense for you to exercise your option, paying $30 each for a block of 100 Sears shares, because you could buy Sears on the open market for 30 or less. But if Sears rises *above* 30, your option will possess real (*intrinsic*) value on the expiration date, because it will enable you to buy Sears stock for 30—less than the going market price.

Should Sears trade at 32 at the end of the option's life ($2 above the $30 strike price of the option), you would break even. Your option would expire with an intrinsic value of $2—exactly what you paid for it. You would double your money if Sears rises another $2 (to 34) and you would triple your money if Sears tacked on yet another $2 (to 36). In short, a $6 gain in Sears shares would fetch you a 200 percent profit (a 3 for 1 return).

The same analysis applies with put options, except that the option builds up intrinsic value as the price of the underlying asset (Sears stock, for instance) drops below the strike price of the option. To illustrate, let's assume that you could buy a put on Sears, exercisable at $30 per share within the next three months, for $2 per share. If Sears dips to 28 at the end of the option's life, you will break even; at 26, you will double your money; at 24, you will triple your money, and so on.

Of course, you pay a price for such spectacular leverage. The probability that you will lose money on any particular option trade is extremely high. Don't fall for the specious argument, advanced by many brokers, that your risk is *limited* when you buy options. True, your risk is contractually limited to the purchase price of the option (the premium). In practice, however, 90 percent of all options expire worthless because the market either doesn't go in the direction the buyer expected or doesn't go as far as expected. For option buyers who hang on to their options until expiration, the chances are 9 in 10 that they will lose their entire investment!

With these long odds, it should come as no surprise that the vast majority of option buyers lose money over time. Nonetheless, by following the Ten Commandments of Speculation—especially the stop-loss rule and the trailing-stop rule—you can substantially improve your likelihood of success. Here are some specific rules for trading options:

- *Never allow a loss on an option to exceed 30 to 40 percent of the purchase price.*
- *Buy "in-the-money" or "near-the-money" options only.* For calls, in the money means that the price of the underlying asset is above the strike price (exercise price) of the option. For in-the-money puts, the underlying asset is trading below the strike price of the option. In-the-money options are much less likely to expire worthless than out-of-the-money options.
- *Close out all options—winners as well as losers—no later than four weeks before the expiration date.* The time value of an option decays rapidly in the last few weeks of the option's life. Even if your option appears to be safely in the money, sell. The clock is ticking, and your risk of losing everything if the market moves sharply against you is mounting rapidly.
- *Buy calls when everyone else is buying puts, and buy puts when everyone else is buying calls.* In the stock market, the best time to buy calls is when the ten-day ratio of calls to puts on the Chicago Board Options Exchange has dropped sharply, to perhaps 1.3 or below (see page 74) at the end of a steep market decline. Buy puts when the call-put ratio has climbed sharply, to 3.0 or above. If you are interested in trading Comex gold options, you might track the gold call-put ratio described in Chapter 8.

For bond options and foreign-currency options, your best trading guide is probably Earl Hadady's *Market Vane* poll, discussed in Chapter 4. (*Market Vane* is also invaluable for the gold trader.) As a contrarian, you will want to buy calls when the vast majority of advisers are bearish and puts when the advisers are bullish—just the opposite of what the crowd is doing.

Selling Options: How the Smart Money Wins Big

Every dollar that option buyers lose flows (after brokerage commissions) into the pockets of option sellers. Since 90 percent of all options expire worthless, it follows that the seller of an option who waits patiently for it to expire stands a 90 percent chance of making money. Speculators with the financial resources to play the seller's side of the options game can build a fortune on those odds.

Selling (or *writing*) options turns off most unsophisticated speculators, for a couple of reasons. To begin with, there doesn't seem to be much money in it. Most stock options sell for $500 or less, and—even under the best of circumstances, assuming the option expires totally worthless—the option writer can't earn more than the price received for the option. Option writing doesn't promise the instant profits of 100, 200, or 300 percent on your investment that are possible when you buy options.

Furthermore, some option-writing strategies pose what appear (superficially, at least) to be grave risks. Think back to our Sears Roebuck example. If you sell a Sears call with a $30 strike price, you have promised to deliver, upon request, 100 shares of Sears for $30 apiece at any time between now and the option's expiration date. You would sell the call if you thought Sears was likely to go down, or at least remain flat, over the life of the option.

But what if Sears goes up sharply instead—to 34, 36, or 38? The call buyer would exercise his option and, if you didn't already own 100 shares of Sears, you would have to go into the marketplace and buy them. (Selling an option without owning the underlying asset is called *naked* option writing.) Because Sears could theoretically soar to infinity, the call buyer's unlimited profit might become your unlimited loss.

Selling naked puts can also saddle you with massive losses. In our example, when you sell a Sears 30 put, you have promised to buy, if asked, 100 shares of Sears at $30 each between now and the option's expiration date. Should Sears go up or remain flat, you will make money. But if Sears drops precipitously (to 26, 24, or 22, say) and the put buyer exercises his or her option, you could end up buying Sears stock from the put owner at a price far above the prevailing market—for a huge loss to you.[3]

To avoid these seemingly horrendous risks, many advisers suggest that option writers stick to selling *covered* calls against stocks, currencies, gold, and other optionable assets that the investor already owns. And it is true that the premiums you collect from covered option writing can boost your income and smooth out the fluctuations in your portfolio.

But naked option writing—the activity that *everybody* is afraid to engage in—can bring the well-financed speculator steady profits of 30 to 50 percent a year, with far less risk than the theoreticians would have you believe. Consider an analogy. A life insurance company would go bankrupt if all its policyholders died at once. But insurance companies survive—and make a potful of money—precisely because they know that the probability of such an occurrence is all but nil. The premiums an insurance company collects more than compensate for the occasional claim the company must pay out.

Likewise, the intelligent option writer recognizes that nine options out of ten expire worthless. As long as the proper steps are taken to limit losses on the few transactions that go against him or her, the probabilities argue that over the long run, the intelligent option writer will rake in far bigger profits than the speculator who buys options in hopes of making a quick killing. Because options are a *wasting asset* with a finite life, time is always on the side of the patient seller—and is always working against the impetuous buyer.

Furthermore, you can significantly pare the risks of option writing by observing the Ten Commandments of Speculation, particularly the stop-loss rule. In general, I suggest that you give your broker a standing order to buy back any option if its market value rises to twice the premium you received for writing it. This procedure will ensure that you never risk more than you stand to gain on an option sale. Unless your stop-loss point is reached, or you have reason to believe that the market is about to swing sharply against you, allow your options to run until expiration. Let time take its course.

In a flat market, you can expand your profits and lower your risk further by selling a put and a call simultaneously at the same strike price. This maneuver is called a *straddle*. In the Sears case, you would have sold a put *and* a call, both with an exercise price of $30, collecting $4 of premiums in the process. As long as Sears stayed above 26 and below 34—a pretty wide band—you would clear a profit. If Sears drifted around dead center for three months (not especially likely, but possible), you would pocket $4 for each straddle, rather than the $2 you would have made if you had simply bet that the stock was going up (write a put) or going down (write a call).[4]

How do you know when to sell options? Sell calls when the crowd is buying—when the call-put ratios are high and most advisers are brimming with optimism. When the crowd is clamoring for puts (the call-put ratios are low) and most advisers are wearing long faces, *sell*

155

puts. As an option writer, you can do the great mass of option buyers a humanitarian favor by giving them what they are secretly craving— a chance to lose money.

Perhaps the best feature of option writing is that it doesn't consume any cash, except when you must buy back your options at a loss. To begin selling options, you can deposit cash or (preferably) interest-bearing securities such as Treasury bills with your broker as margin. Thus, any profits you make on your option writing merely sweeten the yield from your Treasury bills. The option buyer, by contrast, is obliged to pay for his options up front. For the speculator who meets the financial qualifications (many brokerage firms require $50,000 net worth), writing options is less risky than buying them, and far more profitable in the long run.

Commodity Futures: A Stacked Deck

Like options, commodity futures capture a speculator's imagination with the promise of awesome leverage. For example, by plunking down a margin deposit of a little more than $2000, you can buy a contract on the Comex for future delivery of 100 ounces of gold. If the price of gold climbs $20 (roughly a 5 percent gain at current prices), you will double your money; if it drops $20, your stake will be wiped out.

In Chapter 4, I described the contrarian commodity-trading system devised by Earl Hadady, publisher of *Market Vane*. Essentially, Hadady tries to go contrary to the consensus of advisers—and quite often, his recommendations have been amazingly profitable. When he is wrong, it is usually because he bought or sold too soon, before the extreme bullishness or bearishness in the marketplace could force a reversal of prices. As a disciplined short-term trader, however, Hadady sets stop-loss points and thus recognizes his mistakes before they get out of hand. I heartily recommend his service to commodity speculators who are fed up with the whipsaws—and capital losses—that most of the fancy computerized trading systems have generated over the past several years.

Nonetheless, while I think it is possible for a commodity speculator who obeys the Ten Commandments of Speculation to make money, the problem pointed out in the context of option buying also applies to commodity futures. If you buy a futures contract, you are fighting against the clock. As I write, for example, the price of a gold contract expiring a year hence is $45 per ounce higher than the current or *spot* price of

156

gold. Gold for delivery six months from now is $20 an ounce higher than spot.

In other words, the price of gold must rise $20 an ounce within the next six months, and $45 an ounce within the next twelve months, if the speculator who buys those contracts today is simply to break even. Should the price of gold remain steady for the next six months, speculators who put up $2000 to buy a contract today will find that their margin has gone up in smoke. Any interest earned on their margin deposit can't begin to compensate for the erosion of the value of the contract.

Built into the price of most futures contracts is a carrying charge, which represents the cost of buying and storing the commodity until the contract matures. The more distant the delivery month, the greater the carrying charge. For short sellers, the premium of the distant contracts over the nearby contracts is a major advantage; for buyers, it is a major disadvantage. (The reverse order typically prevails in the interest-rate futures. The more distant Treasury bill and Treasury bond futures, for instance, typically sell at lower prices than the nearby contracts. This phenomenon hinders the short seller, but aids the buyer.)

Unless you are planning to trade strictly for the short term (a couple of days to a couple of weeks), the carrying charge will eat deeply into your equity on the *long* (buying) side of most commodities, especially if you speculate on thin margins. Similarly, the wasting time value of an option gobbles up the buyer's premium. If you were wondering why most amateur commodity traders lose money, the carrying charge is undoubtedly a major reason.

Of course, if one of the commodities with a carrying charge looks ready for a fall, you may want to sell it short since prices will tend to drop anyway as the settlement date approaches. Or, if the bond market seems oversold, you may want to buy interest rate futures to take advantage of the tendency of the distant contracts to rise as the settlement date approaches. In either case, the passage of time will benefit you even if the spot market doesn't move at all.

For most speculators most of the time, however, writing options is a much more promising money-making technique than trading commodity futures. The option writer is accumulating income; the commodity trader is dissipating it because of the carrying charge.

Many people feel uncomfortable with leveraged speculations—and rightly so. The speculator who taps other people's money to multiply his own profits always takes a greater risk than the investor who pays cash on the barrelhead. (Don't forget—leverage can multiply your losses, too!) For the speculator who is willing to follow a disciplined approach, however, contrary thinking provides a method for reducing the risks and increasing the rewards of leveraged vehicles such as futures, options, and margin accounts.

But should you fool around with these volatile instruments at all? Only you can resolve that issue, as we will see in Chapter 10.

10

Be Your Own Person, Virginia

Make your decisions based upon what you are, not what you or someone else thinks you should be.

—Harry Browne

Several years ago, an attorney friend from out of state and his family were visiting for a couple of days at our house. Their eldest child and our eldest (both daughters, 2 years old at the time) soon discovered that each wanted to wear the same clothes the other was wearing. If one had a frilly dress on, the other nagged for a frilly dress. If one was wearing red sneakers, the other wanted to wear red sneakers. Finally, my friend, exasperated, bellowed to his daughter, "Be your own person, Virginia!"

As adult investors, of course, we don't need an irate parent to tell us to think and act for ourselves. Nevertheless, I suspect from the letters I receive as an investment adviser that many people are searching for a guru to follow, someone who will take the responsibility for making decisions out of their hands. Too often, brokerage-house clients, customers of bank trust departments, newsletter subscribers, and, alas, even readers of investment books blindly accept an adviser's recommendations without stopping to weigh for themselves the arguments behind the recommendations.

Why are so many people so eager to abdicate responsibility for making their own financial judgments? One factor, no doubt, is the widespread superstition that advisers with prestigious credentials know more about the future than anybody else does. We live in the "Age of the Expert." If we don't understand something, we assume that some-body with a Ph.D. or M.B.A. after his or her name does. Yet the markets, with their unpredictable ways (people are never completely predict-able), succeed in making fools of the experts time and again. Remember how the panel of experts at *Fortune* magazine told us several years ago that Continental Illinois Bank was one of the best-managed companies in America?

Another, and even more powerful, reason why many investors want to be led by the hand is that they believe in the "gospel of the track record." If an advisor has made dazzling profits for his clients recently with a series of accurate predictions or timely market maneuvers, the world assumes that he must know something that nobody else knows. As a result, advisers with a "hot hand" often develop a cult-like fol-lowing of investors who have all but given up thinking critically. Like worshipers, they wait upon their masters' words until, inevitably, the cult leaders' magic touch fails and their clients run up horrendous losses.

Then the disenchanted investors jump ship and sign on with an-other adviser who appears to have found "The Formula." It never occurs to them that they are sacrificing their minds and wills—their own self-respect—to the whims, passions, foibles, and errors of another imper-fect human being. *Everybody* is doing it and *everybody* (for a while) seems to be making money, so they go along—until they discover that, in the end, *everybody* was wrong.

Please understand: I'm not suggesting for a moment that you shouldn't take advice. Others have probably studied the markets more closely than you have. By drawing on their research and experience, you can save yourself the time and money it would take to investigate the uni-verse of investment opportunities yourself. But make sure you apply your own critical judgment to your adviser's *conclusions* and *recom-mendations*. Ask yourself:

- Has this adviser made a logical case for this recommendation, or is he or she engaging in wishful thinking? Does persuasive rhetoric conceal flaws in his or her argument?
- What possible unforeseen factors have been left out?
- Is this adviser merely repeating the conventional wisdom, or is he or she looking behind the obvious to anticipate some surprise that will make prices go up or down?

- Am I taking this advice because I think it is correct or because I believe in the adviser's track record (i.e., he or she has been right in the past)?
- What happens to my investment if this advice turns sour?

Thinking for yourself doesn't mean that you must personally handle every detail of managing your investments. For instance, I believe it is entirely appropriate for investors of moderate means to participate in the stock market through a mutual fund—not because the fund's managers are so much smarter than you are, but because a mutual fund gives you the safety of diversification among fifty or more stocks. If it is a no-load fund, it also slashes your transaction costs (primarily brokerage commissions). But there are hundreds of no-load stock funds to choose from, with radically different investment policies and objectives.[1]

You must decide for yourself which type of fund suits your financial goals—and your temperament. Nobody can determine for you how much risk you are willing to accept and how large a return you wish to seek. Don't let some broker or newsletter writer, who has little to lose by giving risky advice, push you into trading stock options or commodity futures if those tactics will keep you tossing and turning at night. On the other hand, don't allow your friendly bank trust officer to convince you that the only assets a prudent investor should own are blue chip stocks and long-term bonds. If you lack the time or the expertise, by all means hire someone to help you manage your investment portfolio. But see to it that your portfolio reflects your personality and your priorities—not somebody else's.

Risk and Return

The most basic decision you need to make when mapping out an investment portfolio is how much risk you can afford to take. How large a loss could you accept on your investments without jeopardizing your long-term financial goals—buying a home, starting your own business, putting the children through college, assuring yourself a comfortable retirement? Generally, the riskier the investment, the greater the potential return. Although, as I have pointed out several times in earlier chapters, crowd psychology tends to distort investors' perceptions of risk when markets go to extremes of euphoria or despair.

161

Table 10.1 illustrates the spectrum of risks posed by ten popular investments. For this purpose, I am defining "risk" crudely, but simply, as the largest price drop that the asset experienced for any single year (January 1 to December 31) in the six years 1978 to 1983.

Several interesting conclusions emerge from this table. To begin with, as you would expect, the five riskier investments—the bottom half of the list—produced a larger average gain over the five-year period (66.4 percent) than the five safer investments (54.8 percent). But the correlation between risk and reward was far from exact. Money market funds, the least risky investment of all, provided a well-above-average return, for example.

In theory, the safest asset should have yielded the lowest return. But, during times of monetary tension, the market will pay you to stay liquid. Illiquidity is the most striking characteristic of consumer, corporate, and bank balance sheets today. Therefore, I expect that investors will continue to receive above-average returns on money funds, Treasury bills, and other near-cash assets for some time to come—until the worldwide liquidity crisis is resolved and the era of borrow-and-spend comes to a close.

Regardless of your taste for risk, I would suggest that you keep at least 20 to 25 percent of your net worth (apart from your home) in liquid assets for the foreseeable future. If you see a financial thunderstorm

Table 10.1   COMPARISON OF INVESTMENT RISKS

Investment	Largest one-year drop 1978 to 1983 (percent)	Current value of $10,000 invested in 1978
Money market funds	None	$17,944
Single-family home	None	13,865
NYSE stocks	9	20,284
Swiss bank account	11	8,760
Treasury bonds	15	16,557
Commodity basket	18	11,996
Rare coins	24	20,833
Gold	29	20,930
Rare stamps	33	12,903
Silver	57	16,527

blowing up, or if you want to maintain a larger safety margin, you might raise your liquid reserve to 50 percent or more of your net worth. Hold enough cash equivalents to let your mind rest easy.

Another observation I would make about the table is that long-term bonds nowadays are riskier (more volatile) than stocks. Many people, including some readers of *Personal Finance*, still don't want to face up to this unwelcome fact. "Who cares if the bond's market price goes up or down?" a typical questioner will shrug. "I just want to collect the interest and hold the bond to maturity."

Aside from the problem that inflation will erode the value of your principal and interest, you should consider what might happen if you are forced to sell the bond before maturity—perhaps because your spouse comes down with a catastrophic illness, or your neighbor sues you for a million dollars, or some other unexpected contingency interferes with your plans. How would you feel about dumping a bond on the market at 50 cents per dollar of face value—or less? Hundreds of bonds are trading at less than half their face value today (you can survey the wreckage on the bond page of your newspaper), and nearly all of them once sold for par or higher.

The table should also make it clear that gold, silver, rare coins, and stamps aren't the one-way ticket to riches that some hard-money advisers crack them up to be. In fact, if you own any of these tangibles (as I do and encourage you to), you should recognize frankly that by any objective yardstick, they carry major price risks—at least in the short term. To dampen the volatility that these tangibles introduce into your portfolio, it is wise to keep a generous percentage of your assets in stable, short-term interest-bearing paper.

Your Risk Profile

Statistics may seem coldly authoritative, but you should remember that the risk-reward table reflects only the *historical* performance of stocks, bonds, gold, and the like—and then only over a six-year period. Past performance, as mutual fund advertisements say, is no guarantee of future performance. Because the future never exactly resembles the past, it is impossible, in real life, to measure risk with mathematical precision.

Nonetheless, experience suggests that, as a rule, prices fluctuate more widely for some types of assets than for others. Junk bonds bounce around more than Treasury bills. High tech stocks and rare coins take deeper nose-dives than single-family homes. Depending on your tolerance for risk, you should emphasize either more stable or more speculative assets in your portfolio.

To give you some idea of what your risk profile might be, I have prepared the questionnaire below. I invite you to fill it out and score yourself. The average score indicates your risk profile. By matching your risk profile in the left-hand column with the investment strategies in the right-hand column, you can form a rough estmate of how much investment risk you can afford to take. The average risk of all the assets in your portfolio (right-hand column) should equal your risk profile (left-hand column).

Since I have already cautioned you not to place blind faith in any adviser's opinions, I should add that I have based the risk rankings largely on the past performance of each type of investment but also partly on my own "guesstimate" of the future volatility of each asset. Needless to say, I can give no guarantee that all my hunches will prove correct. If you disagree with any of my rankings, I welcome you to amend the table to suit your own perceptions of risk. But I suspect that you will end up ranking most of the investments in the same categories I did, or perhaps one or two steps above or below.

PROFILE ANALYSIS

Directions: Circle the answer that most nearly applies to you. Write that number in the space at right. Then add up the numbers and divide by 9 to get your average score.

AGE   My age bracket is:
(7) under 35   (5) 35–49   (3) 50–57
(2) 58–65   (1) over 65   _____

INCOME   My annual income from all sources is (in thousands):
(1) under 20   (3) 20–29   (5) 30–49
(6) 50–100   (7) over 100   _____

ANNUAL EXPENSES   In relation to income, my annual expenses approximate:
(1) over 95%   (3) 90–95%   (4) 80–89%
(6) 60–79%   (8) under 60%   _____

164

NUMBER OF DEPENDENTS   I currently have these dependents (including nonworking spouse):
(7) 0   (6) 1   (5) 2–3   (3) 4–5   (1) 6 or more   _____

ESTIMATED VALUE OF ASSETS   Market value of my house, cash value of life insurance, savings and investments (in thousands):
(1) under 50   (3) 50–99   (5) 100–249
(7) 250–499   (8) 500 or more   _____

LIABILITIES   My mortgages, installment loans, and long-term debts in relation to assets approximate:
(8) under 30%   (6) 30–49%   (4) 50–69%   (2) 70–90%
(1) over 90%   _____

SAVINGS   I have cash on hand or other liquid assets in savings to equal expenses for:
(1) 2 months   (3) 4 months   (5) 6 months
(6) 1 year   (8) over 1 year   _____

LIFE INSURANCE   My life insurance coverage equals (in thousands):
(6) 250 or more   (4) 150–250   (3) 100–149
(2) 50–99   (1) under 50   _____

HEALTH INSURANCE   My health insurance coverage, counting Medicare but not Social Security disability benefits, includes:
(1) Basic   (3) Major medical plus basic
(5) Catastrophic, major medical, and basic
(7) Catastrophic, major medical, basic, and disability   _____

Score   _____

Risk profile (average score from profile analysis)	Investment strategies
1	Bank savings accounts, money market funds; Treasury bills; universal life policies
2	Bank CDs, government securities, and high-grade corporate and municipal bonds, all with maximum maturity of five years

165

3	Single-family home (for rental); high-grade utility stocks; adjustable-rate bonds and preferred stocks; money market annuities
4	Low P/E stocks and mutual funds invested in low P/E stocks, middle-grade utility stocks; government, corporate, and municipal bonds with maturities up to ten years
5	Gold, quality growth stocks, and mutual funds; convertible bonds and preferreds; variable annuities; tax-sheltered income partnerships; high-grade long-term bonds; foreign bank accounts
6	Aggressive-growth mutual funds; nuclear utilities; silver; mining shares; office and apartment buildings; junk bond funds; option buying
7	Oil-drilling partnerships; junior mortgages; penny stocks; option writing
8	Distressed real estate, high-writeoff tax shelters, margin accounts, and short selling; rare and exotic investments such as stamps, coins, art, antiques, gems, rare books, and other collectibles
9	Commodity futures; stocks and bonds of bankrupt companies

Don't assume, just because your risk profile is 4, 5, or 6, that you shouldn't own any penny stocks, rare coins, or other assets in the higher-risk categories. If you fit into the middle of the scale but your portfolio is heavily weighted with assets in the low-risk categories (1 to 3), you might allocate a modest percentage of your portfolio to high-risk assets. What counts is the *average* risk of your total portfolio, not the risk of each individual component.

An 85-year-old millionaire dowager who keeps 98 percent of her fortune in Treasury bills and 2 percent in penny gold shares is hardly speculating! Even if her penny stocks went to zero, her Treasury bill interest would make up the loss within two or three months. The average risk of her portfolio, according to the ranking system outlined above, would amount to a lowly 1.1.

To take another example, a 40-year-old insurance salesman with an annual income of $40,000 and a risk profile of 4 should ideally strive for an average risk of 4 in his or her total portfolio. Here is how it might be done:

Table 10.2   **RISK PROFILE VS. TOTAL PORTFOLIO**

Investment	Percent of portfolio	Risk category
Bank accounts and money funds	25	1
Universal life policy	5	1
3-year Treasury notes	5	2
Low P/E stocks	10	4
Gold coins	5	5
Convertible bonds	10	5
Aggressive mutual fund	5	6
Nuclear utilities	10	6
Real estate partnership (office buildings)	10	6
Silver	10	6
Naked options	5	7
Average risk*	100	4

*Weighted according to the percentage of the portfolio represented by each asset.

Normally, a person with a risk profile of 4 wouldn't dabble in naked options (ranked 7). But because our insurance salesman had a large reserve of liquid assets (25 percent), he or she could safely afford to put a small percentage of capital to work in naked option writing.

Note, too, that our salesman has spread all risks among eleven different categories of investments. If inflation flares up, the gold coins, silver bullion, and real estate would tend to gain in value. On the other hand, the nuclear utilities and convertible bonds would provide a profit if inflation and interest rates gradually decline. The low P/E stocks and mutual funds should benefit if the economy grows normally. In a deflationary depression, the Treasury notes, bank accounts (or money funds), and universal life policy would maintain our salesperson's purchasing power—assuming that the U.S. government, the banks, and the insurance companies could survive such a cataclysm.

Diversification is the better part of valor in an uncertain world. If neither you nor anybody else really knows how the inflationary debt crisis of our times will be resolved, you shouldn't align your portfolio as if you *did* know. By all means, play the probabilities as you see them. Skew your portfolio toward inflation hedges when the crowd is talking deflation, and toward deflation hedges when the popular opinion is buzzing about inflation. Invest for an economic recovery when the pundits are universally chattering about a depression, and anticipate a slump when *Time* magazine proclaims that all is well.

But never bet all your chips on a single favorite scenario. The markets may not oblige, and what will you do then? Diversification protects you from your own ignorance, stupidity, and greed. As Oliver Cromwell told his Scottish allies in 1650, "I beseech you, in the bowels of Christ, think it possible you may be mistaken!"

Save More, Risk More, Make More

Why can't some people "afford" to live with greater investment risks than others? Personality, broadly defined, has something to do with it, but the profile analysis zeroes in on some more easily measured criteria that reveal your "financial personality"—age, for example. In general, people can accept more risk when they are young, and less when they are old. Working people in their 20s and 30s can usually look forward to a long parade of paychecks before retirement. Hence, younger investors can typically recoup through savings any losses they might incur on high-risk ventures.

By contrast, older investors—especially retirees with social security as their main source of income—find it more difficult to make up a major loss through savings. They are more likely to need all or nearly all their current income for living expenses.

More important than age, however, are one's saving and spending habits. As the questionnaire implies, a person who saves diligently and keeps debts to a minimum can afford to take greater risks (in search of a higher return) than the person who is always financially strapped. The saver has this advantage over the spender almost *regardless* of age or income bracket. Therefore, it is crucial to make a systematic savings program the cornerstone of your long-term wealth-building effort.

Rudyard Kipling, England's poet of empire, once wrote that "any fool can waste, any fool can muddle, but it takes something of a man to save, and the more he saves the more of a man does it make of him." Whether saving is a "manly" virtue or not, many of us find it hard to practice. We know we should be putting more aside, but we don't.

Mark and JoAnn Skousen, in their delightful book, *Never Say Budget!*,* suggest that you can make saving easy by *paying yourself first*. Determine how much you want to save out of your income weekly, monthly, or at whatever interval suits you. (The Skousens recommend salting away 10 percent of your gross take, but I think that some people in the upper income brackets should be able to save considerably more.) Then, when you receive your paycheck, immediately deposit the stipulated amount in whatever savings vehicle you have chosen. *Pay yourself* before you pay any of your other bills—mortgage, utilities, credit cards, you name it. This approach automatically regulates your spending without requiring you to draw up a formal budget. If the money is gone, you can't spend it!

Many people who begin a savings program allow it to lapse after a few months. You can keep your resolution from flagging, the Skousens suggest, by enrolling in a payroll-deduction plan sponsored by your employer. (Often, company profit-sharing plans will match some or all of your contribution, boosting your return substantially.) Or, if your employer doesn't offer such a plan, many mutual funds let you purchase shares through automatic monthly withdrawals from your checking account.

For gold and silver investors, Deak-Perera sponsors a Metals Multiplied program, which allows you to buy a specified dollar amount of precious metals each month. You must deposit at least $1000 to start, but you can set your monthly payments, which aren't mandatory, as low as $100. Deak sends you a bill each month, rather than withdrawing money from your checking account. Commissions are reasonable (2.5 percent maximum), and Deak waives its commission on every sixth purchase to encourage you to stay in the program. (For an application, call Deak at 800-424-1186; in Washington, D.C., 202-872-1233.)

Occasionally, you may feel tempted to raid your savings to pay for some frivolous expense. To help you resist the siren call, the Skousens suggest that you *make it difficult to withdraw your savings*. An Individual Retirement Account (IRA) serves this purpose, since the government imposes a penalty tax if you make a premature withdrawal.

---

*Available for $12.95 postpaid from Alexandria House Books, P.O. Box 9662, Arlington, VA 22209.

Company profit-sharing plans, too, usually discourage withdrawals.

Another savings vehicle that gives you an incentive not to withdraw early is a deferred annuity. With a deferred annuity, any interest, dividends, or short-term capital gains are non-taxable as long as you leave them in the account. If you withdraw more than a small sum within the first few years, the insurance company that issued the annuity will generally charge a 5 to 7 percent penalty. In addition, Uncle Sam socks you with a 5 percent penalty if you withdraw annuity funds before age $59^1/_2$.

The most interesting deferred annuity I have seen lately is Value Guard II, a joint project of Value Line Inc. (publisher of the well-known stock market advisory), and the Guardian Insurance and Annuity Co. (201 Park Ave. S., New York, NY 10003, 212-598-8259). You can sign up for this tax-deferred annuity with as little as $500, and you can make additional contributions of $100 or more at any time.

Value Guard is a variable annuity linked to a mutual fund. (Variable means that your return can go up or down.) The company offers you a choice of four funds: a money market fund, a bond fund, a blue chip stock fund, and the Value Line Centurion Fund, which invests in stocks rated 1 or 2 for timeliness by the Value Line Investment Survey. Over the long pull, stocks in Value Line's top two ranks have outperformed the market by a wide margin, although the service's record in the past year or two has been less than stellar. Since Value Guard imposes no sales charge, 100 percent of your money goes to work immediately.

Slash Your Mortgage in Half

Making extra payments on your home mortgage is a widely overlooked savings technique. Assume for a moment that you are Mr. and Mrs. Average American, buying an average newly built house for $95,000 (roughly the average price). You come forth with the average down payment of about $20,000 and you take out a fixed-rate mortgage for $75,000 at 13 percent for thirty years. Over the life of the $75,000 loan, you will pay a shocking $223,674 in interest. Your $95,000 house will have cost you $20,000 down, $75,000 loan principal, and $223,674 interest for a total of $298,674—more than three times the price you supposedly paid for the house! This is the miracle of compound interest—in reverse.

On the other hand, most lenders allow you to make optional pre-

170

payments of principal in addition to your required monthly payment. Every dollar of principal that you pay off early saves you interest and shortens the term of your mortgage. In our example, you can effectively earn 13 percent a year, compounded monthly, by making extra principal payments on your mortgage. Few investments as safe as your home feature such a high return.

Table 10.3 shows how much interest you can save—and how far ahead of schedule you can extinguish your mortgage—if you slip a few extra dollars in with your monthly mortgage payment. Once again, I am assuming a $75,000 loan for thirty years at 13 percent.

For some reason, this idea drives real estate agents wild. When I first intimated to readers of *Personal Finance* that they could slash their mortgage costs in half by prepaying some of the principal, I received almost a dozen letters from distraught realtors who had one objection or another to the plan. Of course, real estate agents aren't going to be pleased with a scheme that encourages people to stay put and pay off their debts rather than "trading up" every couple of years. After all, how does a realtor bring home the bacon?

Making extra payments on your mortgage won't benefit you if your mortgage was written years ago at a low interest rate (less than 9 percent, say). Furthermore, if you follow this program, your tax deduction for mortgage interest will slowly ebb away, which is a minor drawback, since you can always generate write-offs by making other tax-sheltered investments. Even if you expect to move within a few years, the extra principal payments will make the equity in your present home grow

Table 10.3   PREPAYMENTS OF HOME MORTGAGE PRINCIPAL

Optional monthly payment	Years and months to pay off	Interest saved
$ 25	23 years 4 months	$ 59,372
50	19 years 11 months	88,438
100	16 years 1 month	119,252
150	13 years 9 months	137,032
200	12 years 1 month	149,375
300	9 years 10 months	165,375

faster so that you will probably qualify to buy a more expensive home next time.

Before you start paying down your mortgage, however, remember that you can't withdraw your money, except by selling the house or taking out a home-equity loan. Moreover, making optional payments doesn't free you to skip your regular payments—if you lose your job, for instance. Be sure to build up your holdings of liquid assets (money funds, Treasury bills, and so on) before trying to bulldoze your mountain of mortgage debt.

In the 1970s, the heyday of borrow-and-spend, paying off your mortgage early wasn't chic. Thrift in general wasn't chic. (Did you ever see a *Time* magazine cover on "The Savings Boom"?) But, unnoticed by most people, high interest rates have been changing the economics of saving and spending. Savers are no longer the suckers—not when they can earn 13 percent on their money in a low-inflation environment.

Someday, the crowd will rediscover the virtues of saving, probably *after* a nerve-wracking deflationary crash has driven the prime rate back down to 2 or 3 percent. For now, however, only a minority of Americans—contrarians by instinct—recognize that saving, not borrowing, is the key to getting ahead financially in the volatile 1980s. I'm not saying that inflation has ended, or will end at any time soon. I merely contend that interest rates have risen to the point where saving makes more sense than borrowing for the person who wants to accumulate wealth over the long term.

If you grasp this insight, you will undertake a systematic savings program and invest your savings in a liquid, well-diversified portfolio that reflects your taste for risk. With patience and persistence, you can put all your long-term financial goals within your reach, whether your ambition is to buy a new home or a vacation hideaway, launch your own business, educate your children, or enjoy retirement to the fullest.

Epilogue
It Pays to Be Contrary

I find more and more that it is well to be on the side of the minority, since it is always the more intelligent.
—Johann Wolfgang von Goethe

Contrary thinking, as I have tried to show throughout this book, isn't some kind of negative philosophy for kooks and cranks. Rather, being a contrarian encourages you to stretch your mind and envision possibilities that others don't yet see. Contrary thinking is really nothing more than *thinking for yourself*—one of the highest privileges granted to the human species.

Lower animals live almost entirely according to instinct. They eat, sleep, mate, and migrate without reflecting on what they are doing. And, indeed, since human beings share some psychological characteristics with the rest of the animal kingdom, we often act on instinct, too—for better or for worse. Put us in a crowd, and we will frequently yield to the emotions and impulses of the herd. As Humphrey Neill pointed out (and as every demagogue down through history has known), "A crowd never reasons, but follows its emotions; it accepts without proof what is 'suggested' or 'asserted.' "[1]

But a unique feature of our humanity is that we can also rise above the crowd. Individuals can reason. In Neill's words, "A 'crowd' thinks with its heart . . . while an individual thinks with his brain."[2] Unlike the other animals, we can ask *why* (or why not). It would never occur to a Canadian goose and her gander, for example, to debate whether they should fly south for the winter. The herd instinct, a collective

173

feeling, would decide for them. Human beings, on the other hand, can give you *reasons* why Miami or Toronto is a better place to spend the winter.

Contrary thinking is a philosophy that exalts the individual over the undifferentiated masses. In a crowd, we feel driven to imitate others. We are afraid to be the oddball. Ironically, however, it is always the "intelligent minority"—the few individualists in the crowd—who set the pattern that the rest of the crowd follows. In 1964, the Beatles were the nonconformists who wore long hair when the masses of men preferred butches and flattops. By 1970, *everybody* had changed styles. Long hair was no longer a mark of individuality but of conformity.

Thus, the essence of contrary thinking—and contrary investing—is to be a trend *setter*, rather than a trend *follower*. All the great trailblazers of history were contrarians who broke out of the narrow mindset of their contemporaries (and often had to face ridicule or persecution for their trouble). Einstein was written off as a slow learner by his second-grade teacher. Dr. Jenner was attacked by mobs for vaccinating people against smallpox. Luther was excommunicated. Socrates was poisoned.

Of course, you may not go down in the history books as a hero or a genius like one of those luminaries. As an investor, your goal is more modest—to make money. But the route to investment success is the same course they charted:

- Think for yourself.
- Don't settle for pat answers.
- Challenge the conventional wisdom. Be skeptical of *experts*.
- Look beyond the obvious.
- Steer away from fads.
- Control your emotions, especially fear and hope.
- When the truth is unpleasant, don't try to ignore it. Admit your mistakes while there is time to correct them. Beware of self-deception.

I can't guarantee that you will make a fortune by adhering to these precepts, nor can I assure that you will never suffer a loss. But these principles will give you a far better chance of investment success than all the academic degrees you can earn and all the computer programs you can buy. *Attitude* is everything!

What Is Stopping You?

Candidly, we must all admit that too often we unthinkingly embrace the opinions and prejudices of others, usually out of laziness, or a lack of courage or imagination. In the investment markets, we wait until we notice that others are making handsome profits before we buy (after prices have already gone up) and we wait until we observe that others are losing big money before we sell (after prices have already dropped).

In retrospect, our crowd following can make us look foolish, like the emperor who finally acknowledged to himself that he wasn't wearing any clothes. Why did so many of us buy stocks at the blowoff peak in June 1983 when we had refused to buy them at the panic bottom in August 1982? Why did others among us jump into gold at $850, only to sell in disgust at $300? Because we were allowing the crowd to do our thinking for us. We had set our minds on autopilot. Emotionally, it was easy to go along with what nearly everyone else seemed to be advising and doing. It was also a mistake.

To be a trend setter at a major market turning point is sometimes lonely and uncomfortable, even scary. (The more frightened you feel when going against the crowd, the better your investment decisions will probably turn out to be.) People will wonder why you are behaving so strangely, and you may need to deflect a few smirks and guffaws. But contrary investors take the joshing in stride because they know that the odds are running strongly in their favor. In due time, their daring is likely to be vindicated—spectacularly. Their goal is to remain cool, logical, and detached when everyone else is fired up, irrational, and obsessed with the day-to-day, hour-to-hour meanderings of the market. Although they may look crazy for the short term, they are confident that they will enjoy the last laugh.

To prevent your confidence from melting at market extremes, you must *train yourself* in the habit of contrary thinking. For most of us, it doesn't come naturally, even though we can see the logic of a contrarian approach. Learn to treat bad news as good news, and vice versa: Take a cheerful attitude after prices have fallen sharply (because the ultimate bottom is approaching) and grow cautious after prices have risen steeply (because the final peak is drawing near).

Remember that the degree of risk in the market is exactly the opposite of what the crowd—and your emotions—are probably telling you. As the market approaches a low, the chances that a new buyer will lose money vanish to zero, even though most people are too frightened to buy. Likewise, as the market nears a top, the odds that a new buyer will lose money mount to 100 percent, even though most people are too greedy to sell.

Reading widely (and critically) can help you develop your own independent viewpoint. For the budding contrarian, I recommend that you pay special attention to books and periodicals that take an untrammeled, maverick approach to economics, the investment markets, and human nature. The publications listed in the resources section at the end of this book will sweep the cobwebs out of your mind and give you a refreshing alternative to the dogmas you hear repeated daily in the mass media.

After you have practiced thinking "contrarily" for a while, you will be amazed at how many fine investment opportunities (both buying and selling) present themselves throughout the year, every year. Crowds gather regularly in the stock market, the bond market, the commodity market, the metals market, the real estate market, and every other market. If you know how to recognize the symptoms of crowd hysteria, you can roll up profits with a contrarian strategy in any market you choose.

A Strategy for All Seasons

The insights of contrary opinion apply to any type of investment, and any reasonably intelligent person can put them to work. But the greatest beauty of contrary thinking is that it never goes out of date. It is a philosophy you can take with you for a lifetime. Growth-stock fads may come and go. Gold may skyrocket, or crash and lie dormant for years. Depressions, inflations, wars, revolutions, elections, etc., may transform the economic and political landscape. Yet, through it all, contrary thinking will keep you ahead of the crowd.

I'm not so naive as to suppose that all of the contrary indicators discussed in this book will continue to send off reliable signals into the distant future. In fact, if too many people begin to pay attention to any particular indicator (such as the ASA put-call ratio or the *Time* magazine cover theme), it will probably lose some of its effectiveness. (The markets always do whatever is necessary to frustrate the greatest number of investors!) As a result, contrary investors will be impelled from time to time to develop new barometers of crowd sentiment.

But you needn't worry that someday contrary thinking will cease to be profitable, allegedly because everyone will have become a contrarian. Human nature never changes. As long as the herd instinct is with us, people will tend to follow the leader—especially when the leader seems to know what the future holds. Groupthink is alive and well in today's society. If you doubt it, remember Cabbage Patch.

By reading, and watching, and listening critically, you will begin to sense when a crowd is forming—when public opinion about economic or investment issues is growing too lopsided. "I know insanity when I see it" was how a California high tech executive described the price at which his company's stock went public a couple of years ago. (He shrewdly dumped huge blocks of shares near the 1983 peak.) You will react the same way at important market turning points.

When a calm, dispassionate analysis suggests to you that the market has gone crazy, you are probably right! *Don't* wait for others to reach the same conclusion. *Don't* wait to "see how it turns out." Run for the exits if the market is boiling with euphoria; back up the truck and buy if the market is frozen with panic.

The late Bernard Baruch, who lost millions but nevertheless survived the 1929 crash with most of his fortune, devised a brilliant two-part formula that a sane (but perplexed) investor can call to mind whenever the market seems to have gone off its rocker. In the depths of the depression, Baruch wrote a new foreword for the 1932 edition of Charles Mackay's *Extraordinary Popular Delusions*. He said:

> I have always thought that if, in the lamentable era of the "New Economics," culminating in 1929, even in the very presence of dizzily spiralling prices, we had all continuously repeated, "*two and two still make four*," much of the evil might have been averted. Similarly, even in the general moment of gloom in which this foreword is written, when many begin to wonder if declines will never halt, the appropriate abracadabra may be: "*They always did.*"

The next time some market pundit announces the dawning of a new era after prices have already soared, remind yourself that "two and two still make four"—that value still counts, and trees don't grow to the sky. By the same token, when the market is collapsing week after week and it seems that the declines will never end, reassure yourself: "They always did." There is always a bottom *somewhere*. If you learn to think about the markets with your head instead of your heart, you may yet overtake Bernard Baruch, and perhaps even J. Paul Getty.

Resources

The following books and newsletters are "cobweb sweepers" for the mind. While not all of the authors or publishers would formally label themselves contrarians, their independent-minded approach will help you develop a contrarian attitude toward the markets and life in general.

Books

- *America's Great Depression* by Murray N. Rothbard, Sheed & Ward, Kansas City, MO, 1975 ($15 hardback*). An eye-opening economic history of the depression that lays the blame for the crash at the Federal Reserve's doorstep. Excellent discussion of the causes of the business cycle.
- *The Art of Contrary Thinking* by Humphrey Neill, The Caxton Printers, Caldwell, ID, 1980 ($4 paperback†). Neill coined the term "contrary opinion" and first applied it to the investment markets. A work of genius.
- *The Bible.* The Old Testament prophets, such as Moses, Elijah, and Isaiah, furnish superb examples of men standing alone against the crowd. In the New Testament, Paul and, of course, Jesus are the most prominent contrarians. Christ's dictum in Matthew 7:13–14 is a gem of contrary thinking: "Go through the narrow gate. The gate is wide, and the way is broad, that leads to destruction, and many are going that way. But the gate is small, and the way is narrow, that leads to life, and only a few are finding it" (Beck, translator).

*Available from the Ludwig von Mises Institute, Thach Hall, Auburn University, Auburn, AL 35849.
(Postage extra.)
†Available from Fraser Publishing, P.O. Box 494, Burlington, VT 05402.

- *Contrary Opinion: How to Use It for Profit in Trading Commodity Futures* by R. Earl Hadady, Hadady Publications, Pasadena, CA, 1983 ($37.50). The first systematic attempt to apply contrary thinking to futures trading.
- *The Crowd* by Gustave Le Bon, Viking Press, New York ($3.95 paperback*). Classic study of the mass mind, written in the 1890s. You will see the 1984 presidential campaign on every page.
- *Extraordinary Popular Delusions and the Madness of Crowds* by Charles Mackay, Farrar, Straus & Giroux, New York, 1932 ed. ($8.95 paperback*). Cited at length in Chapter 2, this book chronicles such famous financial manias as the Dutch tulip craze, the South Sea Bubble, and the Mississippi Company.
- *Human Action* by Ludwig von Mises, Henry Regnery Co., Chicago, 1966 ($37.50 hardback†). The greatest economic treatise of our time, by the dean of free-market thinkers. Chapter 20 of Mises' book explains all you will ever need to know about how inflationary government policies cause and perpetuate the boom-bust cycle.
- *The Mystery of Banking* by Murray N. Rothbard, Richardson & Snyder, New York, 1983 ($19.95 hardback†). Why the fractional-reserve banking system is inherently unstable and inflationary.
- *The Richest Man in Babylon* by George S. Clason, E. P. Dutton Co., New York, 1978 ($6 paperback). How to get off the borrow-and-spend treadmill and enjoy true financial security.

Newsletters

- *Personal Finance* (1300 N. 17th St., Suite 1660, Arlington, VA 22209, $94 per year). Richard E. Band, editor. The nation's largest investment newsletter. Articles by more than fifteen contributing editors in different areas of expertise. Strong contrarian flavor.
- *Analysis & Outlook* (P.O. Box 1167, Port Townsend, WA 98368, $32). R. W. Bradford, editor and publisher, is one of the few coin

*Available from the Ludwig von Mises Institute, Thach Hall, Auburn University, Auburn, AL 35849.
(Postage extra.)
†Available from Fraser Publishing, P.O. Box 494, Burlington, VT 05402.

dealers who will advise you not only to buy rare coins but also to *sell* them.

- *The Contrary Investor* (P.O. Box 494, Burlington, VT 05402, $60). James L. Fraser, editor. Philosophical and humorous. Concentrates mostly on the stock market, but offers commentary on economic, social, and political trends as well.

- *Deliberations* (P.O. Box 182, Adelaide St. Sta., Toronto, Ont. M5C 2J1, $215). Editor Ian McAvity combines technical analysis, fundamental analysis, and contrary opinion to arrive at his views of the stock market, bonds, precious metals, and currencies. Outstanding charts.

- *DJH Analysis* (P.O. Box 977, Crystal Lake, IL 60014, $125). Donald J. Hoppe, editor. Hoppe is a skilled contrarian who has called many important market turns in stocks, bonds, and metals. Especially recommended for history buffs; Hoppe frequently draws parallels with manias and crashes of the past.

- *Free Market Perspectives* (P.O. Box 471, Barrington Hills, IL 60010, $95). Alexander Paris, editor. Examines the economy and markets from the perspective of the Austrian school of economics.

- *Growth Stock Outlook* (P.O. Box 9911, Chevy Chase, MD 20815, $95). Charles Allmon, editor. Only newsletter on growth stocks that has survived bull and bear markets for two decades.

- *Investing in Crisis* (1300 N. 17th St., Suite 1660, Arlington, VA 22209, $195). Edited by Douglas Casey, a maverick who defies classification. Covers a host of markets from stocks and bonds to cellular-radio franchises and Hong Kong real estate. Casey forthrightly advocates speculation; he is especially fond of penny mining stocks. An original thinker who often shocks and always entertains.

- *Investors Intelligence* (Larchmont, NY 10538, $84). Michael Burke, editor. Publishes the original stock market sentiment index. News on insider trading, extensive quotations from a broad cross-section of market advisories.

- *Market Vane* (61 S. Lake Ave., Pasadena, CA 91101, $345). Edited by Earl Hadady. Weekly sentiment index for commodity futures, plus occasional commentary on economic issues.

Notes

Chapter 1
1. *Manchester Union Leader* (NH), Dec. 2, 1983.

Chapter 2
1. Ludwig von Mises, *Human Action*, Henry Regnery Co., Chicago, 1966. (See especially Chapter 20.) For an easier introduction to the business cycle, see Murray N. Rothbard, *America's Great Depression*, Sheed & Ward, Kansas City, 1975, chap. 1.
2. Charles Mackay, *Extraordinary Popular Delusions and the Madness of Crowds*, Farrar, Straus & Giroux, New York, 1932 edition, p. 89. (Paperback edition still in print; see resource list, p. 179.)
3. Ibid., p. 94.
4. Ibid.
5. Ibid., p. 95.
6. Ibid., p. 94.
7. Ibid., p. 95.
8. Ibid.
9. Ibid., p. 14.
10. Ibid., p. 19.
11. Ibid., p. 24.
12. Ibid., p. 50.
13. Ibid., p. 52.
14. Ibid., p. 55.
15. Ibid., pp. 55–56.
16. *Growth Stock Outlook*, Oct. 15, 1983, p. 1.
17. John Kenneth Galbraith, *The Great Crash*, 3d ed., Houghton Mifflin, Boston, 1972, p. 15.
18. Ibid., p. 82, quoting from Frederick Lewis Allen, *Only Yesterday*, Harper & Brothers, New York, 1931.
19. Ibid., p. 75.
20. Ibid., p. 31.

Chapter 3
1. Bruce Herschensohn, *The Gods of Antenna*, Arlington House, New Rochelle, NY, 1975. Don Kowet keeps up the drumfire against CBS in *A Matter of Honor*, Macmillan, New York, 1984.
2. *Barron's*, Mar. 7, 1983.
3. *Wall Street Journal*, Oct. 4, 1974.
4. Ibid., Sept. 30, 1974.
5. Ibid., Dec. 6, 1974.
6. Ibid., Aug. 13, 1982.
7. Ibid.
8. Ibid., Nov. 21, 1980.
9. Ibid., June 20, 1983.
10. Ibid., June 23, 1983.
11. Ibid., Jan. 17, 1980.
12. Ibid.
13. Ibid., Jan. 18, 1980.
14. *Western Mining News*, June 25, 1982.
15. *Barron's*, July 9, 1984.
16. Ibid., July 30, 1984.
17. Ibid., March 7, 1983.

Chapter 4
1. R. Earl Hadady, *Contrary Opinion: How to Use It for Profit in Trading Commodity Futures*, Hadady Publications, Pasadena, CA, 1983, p. 41.
2. Ibid., p. 42.
3. *Wall Street Journal*, Jan. 10, 1983.
4. Ibid., July 25, 1983.
5. Ibid., Jan. 23, 1984.

Chapter 5
1. Stocks purchased by chief executive officers do best; stocks sold by directors do worst. Kenneth Nunn et al., "Are Some Insiders More Inside Than Others?" *Journal of Portfolio Management*, Spring 1983.

Chapter 6
1. David Dreman, *Contrarian Investment Strategy*, Random House, New York, 1979; updated as *The New Contrarian Investment Strategy* in 1982.
2. Ibid., p. 245.
3. William J. Grace, Jr., *The Phoenix Approach*, Bantam Books, New York, 1984. This book offers guidance on how to recognize value in a bankrupt company.
4. Lowell Miller, *The Perfect Investment*, E. P. Dutton, New York, 1983.

Chapter 7
1. *New York Times*, March 10, 1980.
2. Invests in U.S. Treasury bills only.

Chapter 8

1. An excellent reference for readers who wish to study gold's long-term record as an inflation hedge is Prof. Roy Jastram's book, *The Golden Constant*, John Wiley & Sons, New York, 1977.
2. Several good books have been written on how to invest in distressed real estate, including *Nothing Down* by Robert G. Allen (Simon & Schuster, New York, 1981), and *How You Can Become Financially Independent by Investing in Real Estate* by Dr. Albert J. Lowry (Simon & Schuster, New York, 1977).
3. Dr. John Wesley English, *The Coming Real Estate Crash*, Arlington House, New Rochelle, NY, 1979.

Chapter 9

1. *DJH Analysis* (P.O. Box 977, Crystal Lake, IL 60014, $125), June 1984.
2. The options exchanges publish a number of helpful booklets for budding speculators. For information on stock options, contact the Options Clearing Corp. (200 S. Wacker Dr., Chicago, IL 60606, 312-322-6200); bonds, the Chicago Board of Trade (LaSalle at Jackson, Chicago, IL 60604, 312-435-3558); gold and silver, the Commodity Exchange, Inc. (4 World Trade Center, New York, NY 10048, 212-938-2900); foreign currencies, the Philadelphia Stock Exchange (1900 Market St., Philadelphia, PA 19103, 215-496-5000).
3. A minor consolation when you are writing puts is that the price of the underlying asset (Sears stock, for instance) can never go below zero. Hence, your risk as a put writer *is*, in a sense, *limited*.
4. For a detailed discussion of options strategies, see Max G. Ansbacher, *The New Options Market*, Walker & Co., New York, 1982.

Chapter 10

1. A comprehensive reference on no-load funds is Sheldon Jacobs's annual *Handbook for No-Load Fund Investors*, available for $29 from The No-Load Fund Investor Inc. (P.O. Box 283, Hastings-on-Hudson, NY 10706). This book lists ten-year performance records for more than 500 funds, together with addresses, phone numbers, minimum investment, shareholder services (such as IRAs and telephone-redemption privileges), and a brief description of the fund's policies and objectives. If you don't care about the performance figures, you can get fund addresses and other basic information from the annual directory of the No-Load Fund Association (11 Penn Plaza, New York, NY 10001), $2.

Epilogue

1. Humphrey Neill, *The Art of Contrary Thinking*, The Caxton Printers, Caldwell, ID, 1980, p. 10.
2. Ibid., p. 3.

Index

187

Bankruptcy, bankrupt companies,
98–100
Banks, credit and money supply,
17–19, 20, 21–22, 25–26, 28–29
Barron's, 33, 43, 78
closed-end bond funds, 114
Market Laboratory, 70–71, 74
options figures, 75, 136, 137, 138
Baruch, Bernard, 18, 177
Batterymarch Financial Management
(Boston), 12
Beatles; Beatlemania, 10, 174
Bible, the, 179–180
Blanchard, James U. & Co., 131
Blunt, John, 25
Bonds, 112–114, 122, 143, 149, 153,
161, 163–164, 165, 166, 167,
171
convertible, 114–116
silver-indexed, 116
(*See also* Treasury bonds)
Book value, company, 95, 99
Boom and bust cycles, 7–8, 15–19,
35–36
symptoms of dying boom, 29–30
(*See also* Manias; Newsletters;
Polls; Stock market timing)
Boston Company Special (mutual
fund), 81
Bradford, R. W., 142, 180
Braniff airlines, 12
British sovereign, 131
Brokers (*see* Advisers)
Brougham, Lord, 17n
Browne, Harry, 159
Burke, Michael, 52, 181
Business Week, 32, 33–34, 45
Buy-and-hold strategy, 81–83, 87
Buying climax, 39

C

Cabbage Patch dolls, 10, 30, 177
California real estate speculators,
1970s, 19–20, 139
Call-put ratios, 74–76, 128–130,

136–138, 151–153, 155–156,
176
Callahan Mining, 138
Campbell Red Lake, 138
Capital gains tax, 86, 150, 170
Capital Preservation Fund, 122
Carter, Jimmy; Carter administration,
45, 111
Casey, Douglas, 44–45, 181
CBS news reporting, 31
Charts, value of, 146–147
Chase Manhattan Bank, 121
Chicago Board of Trade, 75, 76, 112
Options Exchange, 153
Chicago school of economics, 124
Chrysler, 89, 98, 99, 113
Citibank (N.Y.), certificate storage
programs, 135
Citibank South Dakota, 121
Clason, George S., 180
Clayton Brokerage, 52
Cleveland Electric Illuminating, 97,
117
Closed-end funds, 27, 113–114
Closed-end investment companies,
27
Coeur d'Alene Mines, 138
Cohen, Abraham W., 48, 52
Coin dealers, 131, 141–142
Coins:
junk silver, 132–135
rare, 141–142, 162, 163, 164, 166,
167, 180
Coleco Industries, 15–16, 151
Collectibles and tangibles, 126, 138,
141–142, 162–163, 166
Comdisco, 16
Comex (*see* Commodity Exchange)
Coming Real Estate Crash, The (English), 140–141
Commercial banks, money and credit
supply, 17–19, 21–22, 25–26
Commodities futures, 57–59, 61,
144, 156–158, 161, 162, 166,
181
Commodity Exchange (Comex—New
York), 41, 54, 128, 153, 156